BUM STEERS

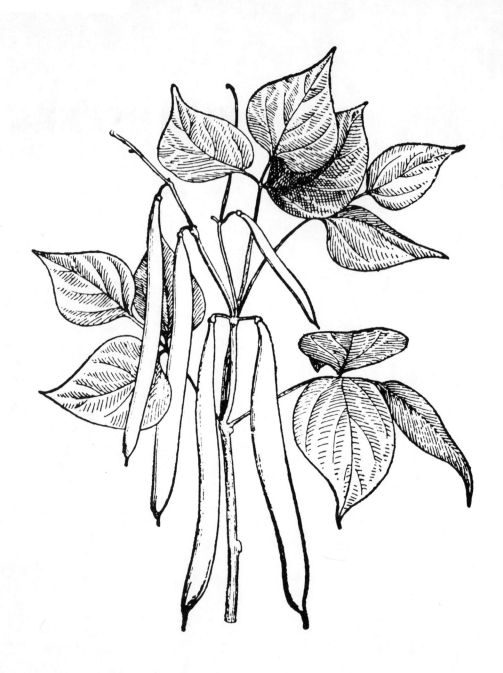

BUM STEERS

*How and Why to
Make Your Own Delicious High Protein
Mock Meats, Fake Fish & Dairyless Desserts
and Avoid Useless Calories, Cholesterol,
Sodium Nitrite
Salmonella, Trichinosis*

&

High Prices

by FRANCES SHERIDAN GOULART

THE CHATHAM PRESS, OLD GREENWICH, CONNECTICUT

For Ron,
the man
whose one meat
this
book
was.

Library of Congress Catalog Card Number: 75-4499
ISBN: 85699-113-9 (hardcover edition)
*   85699-114-7 (papercover edition)*

Printed in the United States of America
by the Murray Printing Co.

The illustrations, used by the kind permission
of the McGraw Hill Book Co., were done by
Mrs. Elizabeth Burckmyer for Fieldbook of
Natural History, by E. Laurence Palmer,
copyright, 1949.

CONTENTS

INTRODUCTION

Americans may still be the world's burger kings, but the burger (along with the steak and the chop) is fast becoming an endangered species, with good reason.

The American Heart Association, for instance, feels that a one-third reduction in our annual average per capita intake of 250 pounds of meat (the highest in the world) would measurably curb the rising incidence of coronary disease in this country. One good-sized portion of steak, says the Federal Government's Heart Disease Resources Agency, can yield as much as 50 grams of saturated fat — twice the total daily intake of such fats recommended by that agency.

Even for that American institution, the hotdog (of which we consumed more than 15.5 billion in 1974), there is increasingly little to be said. According to the U.S. Department of Agriculture figures, the average frank is only 12 per cent protein and 28 per cent fat (50 per cent more fat than 35 years ago). And convicted carcinogens such as sodium nitrite comprise half the quantity of curing agents used in preparing such "convenience meats" and cold cuts.

The National Academy of Sciences says the steak-loving American has for the last twenty years been consuming as much as 15 per cent more meat protein than his body can efficiently handle. The Academy, along with many nutrition experts, suggests that this heavy meat-eating can be considered a form of malnutrition.

Knowing all this, we are surely ready for a steer in another direction, perhaps as part-time herbivores living a lot lower on the hog and a little higher on the peanut, the soybean and other direct food crops. It is estimated that, if we lived on vegetable protein alone, Kansas, Nebraska, and the two Dakotas could feed the entire United States (the state of Kansas now produces more soybeans than the Soviet Union and all of Europe together). As writer Richard Rhodes has observed, we use the world's cheapest source of protein (soybeans) to grow the world's most expensive (cattle).

Mahatma Gandhi called vegetables "innocent foods." Aside from a few curious examples (e.g. coconuts, which yield significant amounts of saturated fats), how could you regard a Brussels sprout or a Polish pickle as anything but blameless? They are admirably low in all the things meat is high in — calories, cholesterol and cost. Some vegetables might even be considered wonder-foods. The chili pepper, for instance, has the apparent ability to lower blood cholesterol levels and also to supply vitamin A in an amount rivalled only by beef liver. Garlic is such a powerful natural germicide it is known in some quarters as "Russian penicillin."

"Vegebutchering" — the subject of this book — is the art of making "mock meats" from the good beans, greens and grains of the plant world. It purposefully meets the standard of the National Academy of Sciences, which says: "A vegetarian can be well nourished if he eats a variety of plant food and gives attention to crucial nutrients."

Just one example of how vegetables can supply "crucial nutrients": The sunflower seed is 25 per cent protein. In seedmeal form, the proportion is 50 per cent, making sunflower seeds a protein source comparable to meat. Unusual in a plant food, sunflower seeds also supply generous amounts of vitamin D, which with B_{12} and calcium is usually thought to be in short supply, if present at all, in plant protein.

Vegetables, unlike meat, supply dietary roughage, deliver few calories (84 in a whole pound of summer squash), and at the same time yield goodly, though non-concentrated, amounts of the harder-to-get amino acids which are the building blocks of protein.

In addition, there are some tangible rewards for *not* bringing home the bacon. Not only do non-meat-eaters tend to be thinner, but they are often richer as a result of their dietary practices. Studies indicate that a family of four non-meat-eaters can eat protein-rich dishes based on plant foods for less than 30 cents a portion, realizing a saving in expenditure for proteins of roughly 25 per cent.

In fairness to the fatted calf, it must be conceded that meat is not without its virtures, being virtually free of carbohydrates and supplying high-quality protein with an amino acid distribution pattern superior to that found in any single direct food crop. Nevertheless, a similar complete protein pattern can be provided by the careful combination of vegetable foods. Cereal grains, such as whole-wheat, in combination with, say, pinto beans will yield complete protein equivalent to that of the muscle meats of the usual meat-eater's diet.

There is another reason besides health and personal finances for turning to

8

sources other than meat for nourishment. As humanitarians, we cannot be unmoved by the thought that if every American ate only one less hamburger per week, eventually 12 million tons of grain each year would be freed from the fattening of cattle and could be used to feed 60 million people instead.

So powerful are the arguments for avoiding meat that it is not at all surprising that there are many who are convinced that the human system was never intended to handle a carnivorous diet, and that man was originally a complete herbivore. While the term "vegetarianism" is relatively new, the practice is not. Mock-meat making dates back to early Buddhist sects and indeed may be as old and as venerable as the soybean itself. The practice of it, requiring nothing more exotic than a blender, a bag of grain, a sack of beans, fresh greens, spices and a desire for discovery, could hardly be simpler. What's ahead for dinner? Let a parsnip rather than a pork chop lead the way.

A WORD TO THE WISE READER

To serve roast beef, you don't have to know how to make a cow. But to get a silk purse (in the form of a mock pork chop) out of a mock sow's ear takes some special knowledge. Thus, before going on to the recipes, the reader is urged to go through the basic training presented in the first two chapters. Here you will find the fundamental details for preparing the stuff of which mock meats are made. This stuff includes tofu, gluten, bean paste, seedmeat, etc., plus such ingredients as Mock Milk, a series of Mock Marinades and an especially valuable seasoning called Vegebutcher salt.

Any other ingredients that sound unfamiliar should be readily available at all natural-food stores, but if they are not, mail-order sources are listed at the end of the book in the section called STEERAGE.

BUM STEERS

ON THE BLOCK: MAJOR MOCK-MEAT-MAKING SUPPLIES

TOFU

Tofu is simply fresh soybean "cheese" prepared from dried soybeans, from soy milk, or soy flour. Called "meat without bones" by the Chinese, it contains 2 1/2 times as much protein as meat while costing only one third as much to prepare. Puddinglike and bland in flavor, it is similar in texture to cream cheese yet more delicate. Tofu contains 21 of the 23 known amino acids, is low in starch and carbohydrates and crude fiber. It is rich in calcium and phosphorus and is one of the best sources of potassium. This soybean "meat" requires no cooking after preparation and may be used cubed, chunked, pureed, slivered, mashed, and in combination with almost any ingredient imaginable. It may even be frozen.

Note: Ready-to-go Tofu may be bought in some specialty shops, where it may be found as: *Dow Foo* or *Suey Dow Foo, Kinugoshi, Age* or *Nama-age.* In this form it usually comes with a mild vegetable preservative, if you are concerned about chemical additives.

Composition of Tofu per 100 grams

Water	85.1 gm.
Protein	7 gm.
Fat	4.1 gm.
Carbohydrates	3 gm.
Ash	0.8 gm.
Calcium	100 mg.
Phosphorus	95 mg.
Iron	1.5 mg.
Thiamine	0.06 mg.
Riboflavin (B²)	0.05 mg.
Niacin (B³)	0.40 mg.

THE SOYBEAN

The finest variety is the *bonsei* and the finest Tofu is made from green soybeans. So supernutritious is the soybean that a pennysworth of it added to a 12-oz bottle of cola would produce a drink equal to milk in protein! Soybeans contain 331 calories per 100 gms (about 3 oz), are 40% protein (twice the amount in most beans), 18% fat (unsaturated of course), 25% carbohydrate (that's very modest), and are an outstanding source of potassium, phosphorus and sodium as well as vitamin A (140 units in each 3 oz) and the B vitamins choline and inositol. Soy oil is the major source of polyunsaturates among the fats and oils.

Soybeans come in many protein-rich forms. Soybean granules, for instance, are 50% protein while meat is 25%. Soy protein, however, must be supplemented since it is deficient in some of the essential amino acids. Likewise, the soybean's mineral balance is imperfect. It is high in the dietary iron which cow's milk lacks, but low in the calcium for which the latter is so famous. Thus, because the soybean is rich in phosphorus (which the body needs only half as much as calcium), it should be served in partnership with something that supplies calcium, such as brazil nuts, sesame seeds, blackstrap molasses, carob powder, or, of course, any dairy product.

Soybeans, called "the cow of China," have been an essential food in that country for 4,000 years, and for many thousands of years have provided the sole source of protein for many of the world's peoples. Today the U.S. produces 80% of the world's supply. It is expected that sales of soybean products will rise from today's level of 75 million dollars annually to 2 billion by 1980. Increased consumption of soybean products will, however, necessitate an equally increased intake of foods supplying calcium and zinc owing to the presence in soybeans of substances called phytates which interfere with protein assimilation if taken in excess.

Soybeans are three times as digestible as meat and can (unlike meat) be the basis for virtually any prepared dish: foodstuffs from milk, to cheese, to bread, butter, mayonnaise, and even a superior meat sauce (soy sauce). Commercial refined soybean products, however (soy extenders, texturized soy protein, etc.), lack many essential vitamins and minerals despite the added protein they offer and should be avoided, according to the American Medical Association's Council on Foods and Nutrition.

GLUTEN FLOUR

Gluten flour is made by washing the starch from high-protein wheat flour. It is then dried and ground. Gluten flour is indispensable in baking with soy, rye, buckwheat and other flours low in this dough-forming substance. It is excellent for making gravies and sauces, but is low in minerals and must be supplemented with protein from other sources. It provides about half as much usable protein as soybean flour.

One-third cup of gluten supplies:
Calories 355
Protein 41.6
Fat 1.76
Carbohydrates 43.6
Minerals   No information
& vitamins .... available.

LEGUMES
Peas, Beans and Lentils

All legumes are at least 20% protein, though it is incomplete protein. Unless joined with rice, corn or wheat products, they are a poor nutritional match for a pot roast or even an ice cream sundae (they lack some very essential amino acids like methionine, of which there is only a trace in legumes). Beans are low in cholesterol although most are high in carbohydrates and, for some individuals, seem to have blood-cholesterol-leveling properties. All beans supply respectable amounts of minerals like iron, calcium and phosphorus and are noteworthy for their contributions of vitamins A, C, and especially B to the diet (sprouted beans are especially generous in this respect.) All in all, a hill of beans is not such a bad thing to amount to after all.

Six varieties of beans with markedly different personalities might make up your basic bean cupboard: kidney beans, soybeans, navy, lima and lentil. Or, cranberry, garbanzo, pinto, soy, black-eye, dried pea. Four more combinations are suggested below. Mail-order sources for some of the more exotic varieties are listed in STEERAGE.

(a)   Great Northern beans or navy beans, soybeans, lentils, marrow beans.
(b)   Turtle beans, brown beans, cow peas, soybeans.
(c)   Chick-peas (garbanzos), soybeans, dried lima beans, black-eyed peas.
(d)   Vermont soldier beans (for Boston Baked Beans), Santa Maria beans (Calif.) for chili, Cuban black beans, pink (Mexican) beans, (more nutritious than the navy bean and bigger), soybeans.

Note: Try sprouting some of each type of bean you homestead. The protein patterns of beans, seeds and grains complement each other, thus your germinated garbanzos will make good nutritional company for your sprouted sesame or hard wheat.

VEGETABLES

Animal foods are very poor sources of such essential nutrients as sugars, starches, pectins, hemicelluloses and celluloses, and non-digestible fibers, with the exception of lactose, a sugar found in cow's milk. By contrast, plant foods are easily digested, low in calories (broccoli, for instance, has only 56 calories per pound), and a rich source of phosphorus, iron (all plants contain iron), vitamins C and A, and even E (celery has it, so does fennel), plus the B vitamins (potatoes contain good supplies of B^3 and B^2), and even such wonder-working substances as myrtillin, a nutrient that reputedly stabilizes high blood-sugar levels or keeps them on a normal keel. Leafy green vegetables contain small amounts of many of the hard-to-find amino acids, cucumbers have a protein-digesting enzyme, and dried peas are 22% protein, contain all eight of the most essential amino acids and when sprouted have a flavor similar to fresh peas. Sprouted vegetable seeds are even more abundant sources of vitamins and minerals. Surprisingly, complete protein is found in spinach, peas, kale, broccoli and potatoes (it is found, however, in a nonconcentrated form). And of all the vegetable proteins, potatoes (like brown rice) register the highest biological values (potato starch is also the easiest of all the vegetable starches to digest and assimilate).

Plant foods rich in vitamins are inevitably rich in minerals as well. Thus are they renowned as "protective foods." "The only foods so constituted as to make good the deficiencies of cereal grains, legume seeds, tubers and muscle meats, are plant foods", according to Johns Hopkins University nutritionist E. V. McCollum.

With the exception of vitamin D, vegetables are well endowed with one or more of all the essential vitamins and minerals without which the body could not utilize protein.

Vegetable carbohydrate ranges from 3% (lettuce) to 26% (sweet potatoes) while the dry grains contain 70% starch. The range for fruit is 10 - 22%.

If not organically grown, all vegetables should be washed with soap and hot water, soaked in a strong salt or vinegar water solution, or peeled.

Buy vegetables fresh, in season and in their natural state whenever possible. Supplement your supply with the dried forms wherever possible. Examples: dried mushrooms, dried pepper flakes, dehydrated vegetable flakes, garlic and onion flakes, flaked parsley, chives, shallots, etc.

WHOLE GRAINS

Whole grains contain a substance (nitriloside or B[17]) that increases the body's resistance to degenerative diseases, another responsible for stabilizing and sometimes lowering cholesterol levels (myrtillin, found in oats, barley, wheat), along with a richness of nitrogen that can be hard on the kidneys and a level of the amino acid, lysine (and sometimes isoleucine as well), so low that they never supply complete protein eaten alone.

After wheat, of which there are several kinds, and oats and barley, you still have semolina, buckwheat, millet, rice, of which there are several kinds, bulgur, couscous and others to put in your pot. The protein values of grains vary greatly from a low of 9% (for unbolted yellow cornmeal) to a high of 20% (for the hybrid rye-wheat grain called triticale). In terms of protein yield, that the body utilizes efficiently, whole brown rice reputedly gets a score of 70%. The protein of buckwheat and oatmeal is higher than that of vegetables and nearly comparable to the protein quality of beef.

17

Dark buckwheat flour provides more magnesium than any other whole-grain flour (with millet probably a close second). Oatmeal, curiously enough, because of the gentle manner in which it is milled, is actually in the same class as whole grains such as rice. Rice (the longer grain is richer in protein than the shorter), like millet and barley, is a rich calcium source. Because of its superior digestibility (it is very alkaline) millet deserves a place in your grain pantry. And because of its B vitamins and its modest caloric count, so does buckwheat, hulled or in its whole "groats" form.

Bulgur, known as the rice of the Middle East, is cracked wheat, easy and quick to cook, though such convenience is paid for by a lower B vitamin score. A kin to bulgur is kasha.

Wheat, oats and rye can all be cooked in the same simple manner as rice and the incomplete protein of rice is nicely supplemented by one or the other. Freshly ground whole-wheat (no matter how you cook it) is one of the best organic sources of manganese which is, in turn, related to the absorption of iron into the body. Of all the plant sources, buckwheat protein is the one which most closely resembles animal protein.

Barley, which we should not reserve only for our babies, is rich in calcium and, like millet, highly digestible. It is also an "antique" among the whole grains, dating back to prehistoric times, and so hardy that it grows today in the Arctic Circle. Put your grain pantry together from the following:

(a) Buckwheat groats or kasha, cornmeal, oats or oatmeal, whole-wheat berries, short grain rice.
(b) Bulgur or cracked wheat, millet, barley, semolina, long-grain rice.
(c) A somewhat more exotic selection includes wild rice, couscous, whole rye berries, whole triticale grains.

See Grainola I, in VEGEBUTCHERING, for complete cooking instructions.

NUTS AND SEEDS

Nuts contain more food value per pound than meat, grain or fruit. Some authorities are even on record as saying that one pound of nuts equals approximately two-and-one-half pounds of beefsteak. All nuts are seeds and as such are rich protein, fat and carbohydrate foods. Nut protein in its natural state is very easily digested. Highest in protein are peanuts and almonds, while pecans contain the most fat (70%) and greatest calorie count (3300 per edible pound). Chestnuts, with only 6% protein, have the highest carbohydrate rating (40%) while lowest carbohydrate readings go to the walnut and the pignolia or pinenut. The pinenut, however, is the most alkaline and therefore the most digestible of all nutmeats and is very rich in calcium. Pistachios, unlike walnuts and pecans, are rich in iron and low in natural tannic acid. The black walnut is distinguished as the prime nutmeat source of manganese, the brain- and nerve-building mineral.

Seeds, other than nuts, contain, according to nutritionists, nearly every single food element that has been discovered. They are the highest in protein of all the foods in the vegetable kingdom and contain all of the 10 essential amino acids. Seeds are 20 times richer in phosphorus than fish, provide ample amounts of calcium, and generous amounts of vitamin E and the fatty acids (EFA) which help to emulsify cholesterol in the system.

Buy all nuts and seeds unshelled and unhulled, unsprayed, unbleached and as close to the natural state as possible.

HOW TO COOK NUTS AND SEEDS
Nuts can be crisped at 220°, toasted (dry-roasted) at 300°-325° (never higher). Seeds can be browned in the oven (never higher than 300° and never untended). Because of their high oil content, they are highly perishable, and once chopped, crushed or heated they are even more so; thus refrigeration is a must.

SPROUTED SEEDS
Seedmeat

Of all the ingredients involved in mock-meat making, sprouts (germinated vegetable, nut, bean, dried pea and grain seeds) are certainly top-seeded. Rich in chlorophyll, seeds are a high quality protein food capable of sustaining reproduction throughout successive generations, as the experiments of Dr. Francis Pottinger have demonstrated. Seeds in their "mini-plant" stage contain nearly all the essential food elements, are rich in vitamin E and the entire B-complex of vitamins. (Yale's Dr. Paul Burkholder discovered, for instance, that oats sprouted for 5 days had 500% more B6, 600% more folic acid, 10% more B1 and 1350% more B2 than ungerminated oats). Soybean sprouts, tested for their vitamin C content after 72 hours of germination, (in their unsprouted stage they contain none), revealed as much ascorbic acid, per half cup, as 6 glasses of orange juice, according to tests at the University of Pennsylvania by Dr. Pauline Berry Mack.

Because of the high quality of the enzymes they contain, the starch and protein of sprouts can be unhesitatingly consumed by anyone with any health problem. They are reputedly an antidote for a wide variety of failings, from constipation to poor resistance. Alfalfa seeds, especially, have been helpful in lowering elevated cholesterol levels.

Sprouted-seed protein, according to Ann Wigmore of the Hippocrates Health Institute, Boston, is far superior to animal protein (chick-pea sprouts are especially high in protein). It is purer and, because the sprouting process neutralizes substances called phytates which can block the absorption of minerals and protein, the minerals found in excellent supply and good balance in most sprouts are much easier for the body to assimilate. This same sprouting process also renders all beans considerably less gas-producing.

Vegetable sprouts which you should not eat, because they contain toxic enzymes, include lima beans, tomatoes, potatoes. Among the countless seeds you *can* sprout (and use as "meat" for burgers, meatloaves, casseroles, dumplings, cutlets, etc.) are: mung, alfalfa, wheat, rye, triticale, lentils, garbanzo beans, barley, garden peas, unhulled sesame and sunflower seeds, kidney, pinto and navy beans, radish and mustard seed. A useful rule of thumb to remember is that one pound of seed yields between six and eight pounds of sprouts.

> ". . . Americans constituting only 6% of the world's population, manage still to account for 30% of the world's meat consumption (and thereby get their protein supply far less efficiently or healthfully than those who rely on pulses — peas, beans, lentils — nuts and grains) . . ."
> — Paul R. Ehrlich, *End of Affluence*, Ballantine Books, 1974

ADDITIVES
Natural Preservatives and Other Nutritive Additives for Your Mock-Meat Making.

Note: You need not be reminded to stock salt, pepper, parsley, or prepared mustard. Only the more un-run-of-the-mill supplies are listed below. Those with mail-order sources (see STEERAGE) are starred.*

SALTS, HERBS, SPICES

Dry Mustard: essential, especially in salt-free preparations.

Sea salt: (does not contain the numerous additives found in supermarket table salt).

Szechuan peppercorns*: optional but interesting.

Hickory-smoked salt: lends meaty flavor to pseudo-meats.

Powdered seaweed (dulse or kelp): available in small shakers; a source of 22 major and minor minerals. Can replace salt and/or pepper.

Paprika: a source of ascorbic acid and a pepper substitute.

Pickling Spices, Fines Herbes, Poultry Seasoning, Crab or *Shrimp Boil Seasoning*:* If you don't make your own (recipes later), buy a good commercial version.

Oregano, Savory, Thyme, Marjoram, Basil, Dill: Buy good commercial versions if you don't raise and dry your own.

Flakes of *garlic, onion, horseradish, chili peppers, bell peppers, dehydrated mixed vegetables, mint.*

Organic Seasoning (or Soup) Broth: A nutritious vegetable-based MSG-free powder sold in most health food shops.

Lemon peel: grate, dry and freeze your own supply.

Ginger: peel, grate, dry and freeze your own, using the fresh root.

Horseradish: like the two ingredients above, an essential flavoring agent in mock-meat making. Buy the fresh root and process it yourself.

Horseradish powder: if fresh is not available.

Gumbo file (okra) *powder:* a handy sauce-thickener; a valuable flavoring agent. Optional but interesting.

Seeds: poppy, celery, caraway, sesame, alfalfa, sunflower.

Mushroom powder, dried mushrooms or *mushroom flakes.*

21

Nutritional yeast (also sold as brewer's or food yeast): Find a good-tasting brand. Taste can be even further improved by the addition of small amounts of toasted peanut meal.

Peanut meal*: One of the two richest sources of pantothenic acid (soybeans are the other) and the richest of all nut-protein sources. Buy it raw and toast it yourself. May replace soy meal in recipes.

Soy lecithin granules or flakes: An essential nutrient, the finest source of phosphorus, high in protein. A natural emulsifier for sauces, for baking. Fine source of unsaturated fatty oils.

Peanut butter: Simply peanut meal with oil added. Use for the same reasons you use peanut meal.

Sesame butter (tahini): Commercial versions available, but best to do it yourself (recipe later). A good substitute for dairy butter.

Vegetable oils & butters: Find a good, palatable brand of imported virgin olive oil and buy a large can. It gives a meaty flavor to meatless dishes. Don't refrigerate and do not use to deep-fry. Use corn or peanut oils for deep-frying. Any additive-free blend of vegetable oils is acceptable for general sauteing. Safflower oil, corn and peanut oils are also suitable for all-purpose all-around cooking. Reserve the nut oils for seasoning and use where a special pronounced flavor is desired. Sesame oil (a valuable source of the sulfur-containing amino acids so rare in plant protein) and wheat-germ oil (rich in lysine, the amino acid most often missing from plant proteins) should be stocked in small quantities. You may also want to keep small bottles of avocado, walnut, almond, and pumpkin-seed oil for the taste they lend to dishes. A less expensive alternative, with a pronounced nut flavor, is sunflower seed oil. Soy butter: If you don't make your own, (recipe later), buy a good commercial brand from your health-food store. It's also known as soy oleomargarine.

Miso: Fermented soybean preparation, high in natural concentrated dextrose and protein, for gravy-making, seasoning, flavoring. Its taste in cooked dishes is often described as "chicken-like."

Yeast extract (marmite): A highly beneficial (like all fermented foods) extract derived from food yeast. Use it in addition to, or instead of, miso.

Soy sauce: Invest in a large bottle of the naturally fermented unprocessed variety (no sugar, no salt, no artificial coloring) — i.e., Tamari.

22

Worcestershire sauce: An indispensable browning and flavoring aid. Look for the one brand that is chemical-free.

Tabasco (or any additive-free liquid pepper): Essential flavoring aid.

THICKENERS
For Sauces, Gravies, Soups

Arrowroot: Available commercially as a "flour," or "powder". High in calcium and other minerals (unlike cornstarch and white flour) and easily digested.

Potato flour (or "starch"): A natural nutritious thickener for vegetable-based sauces. Substitute for white flour or cornstarch.

Seaweeds (kelp, dulse, kombu, wakame, nori): Essential for fish-flavored broths and seafood-flavored dishes. One or more types handy to have. High in vitamins and all the minerals, including trace minerals.

Hizichi: a strand seaweed, pleasantly salty, pleasantly fishy, scandalously nutritious. A good fishy spaghetti substitute.

> "Many of these supermarket garlic- and onion-salt seasonings contain MSG with up to 50% salt and in many or most cases, fillers such as flour, starches, hydrolized vegetable protein, various preservatives, shelf life extenders and flavor enhancers . . ."
> — Founder of an organic herb farm.

VEGEBUTCHERING: MASTER MOCK-MEAT RECIPE FILE

PREPARED GLUTEN (WHEAT PROTEIN)

METHOD I
Begin with 8 cups of gluten flour (whole-wheat or unbleached white bread flours may also be used but with less predictable results). Mix with 2 1/2 to 3 cups of water to make a stiff dough. Form into a ball and knead well, about 15 minutes. Let the dough stand under cold water at least 2 hours or longer. Wash out starch by kneading the dough ball, at regular intervals over a period of several hours, and pouring off the starchy water. Replace with clean cold water each time and repeat this procedure until the water runs clear. This is Gluten in its uncooked state. To prepare for baking, roasting, broiling, etc., slice in scallops, cubes, slivers, or whatever form you desire, and poach, in enough water or broth to cover, in a covered saucepan for 30 minutes. Store in the cooking broth before and after any further preparations to prevent drying out.

METHOD II
Use 10 cups whole-wheat flour and 4 cups of unbleached white flour. Mix these together and dissolve 2 tsp salt in 5 cups water. Add to flours to make a soft dough. Knead 20 minutes and let dough sit in a dry bowl uncovered for 40 minutes. Add 10 cups of water and knead, changing water as in Gluten I. Save starchy water for making future loaves of bread. After 5 or 6 rinsings and kneadings, you should have about 5 cups of Gluten. Pull it into 1 inch pieces with your fingers and drop into a kettle containing 12 boiling cups of water. When pieces rise to the top, strain and wash several times in cold water until quite cold. Saute some garlic and/or ginger slices in oil, pour in some soy sauce and simmer with Gluten chunks for 2 hours. Store in this pot-liquor and use as directed in the recipes which follow or in any you prefer. *Note:* you may either

replenish the soy sauce as it simmers away, or let it simmer away if you are not planning to store your supply for long.

INSTANT PREPARED GLUTEN

Add boiling water to rice flour along with 1 tsp baking powder and 1/2 tsp salt for each cup of flour. Knead into a dough. Put into any steamer and steam-cook til dry and light (20 mins or thereabouts). Divide into desired-sized portions.

TOFU (SOYBEAN CURD)

METHOD I
1. Soak 2 or 3 cups dry soybeans overnight (or longer). 3 cups will completely fill 2 quart jars when soaking. Change water at least twice.
2. Liquefy soaked beans in blender until smooth with no grittiness. To prevent overloading the blender, take 1 or 2 cups soaked beans and 2 or 3 cups of fresh water at a time until all the soaked beans have been liquefied.
3. Pour bean puree into a firm cloth sack and squeeze milky liquid into deep (8-qt is best) kettle. Squeeze until pulp in sack is quite dry. With open end of sack held closed so the pulp will not come out, rinse in about 1 pint of water until all milky fluid is thoroughly washed out of pulp. Discard pulp (or reserve for uses mentioned in *Bummers* — see STEERAGE) and put liquid into a well-oiled 8 quart kettle. (You may add water to make up to 6 qts milky liquid if desired.)
4. Bring liquid to a boil, stirring constantly from bottom of kettle to prevent burning. Boil about 6 mins, stirring all the while. Watch carefully.
5. Remove from stove and let cool to 180°.
6. Dissolve 1 tsp of magnesium sulphate (epsom salts) for each cup dry beans in approximately 1/2 cup warm water. Pour this slowly into the boiled liquid which has been cooled to 180°. Let stand until curd is well formed (about 20 mins).
26   7. Pour into colander lined with double layer of cheesecloth to drain. Fold

cheesecloth over top of curd and cover with a lid or saucer smaller than the diameter of the colander. Put a 2 or 3 lb weight on top to expel any remaining whey.

8. Curd should be firm in about 20 minutes, but after half that time it is helpful to set the colander in cool water to hurry along the jelling process. Remove curd by picking up the edges of the cloth and turning Tofu out onto counter. Cut into handy cubes or slices and store in salted water in refrigerator. Change water daily if you don't use Tofu immediately.

METHOD II
Place 3 cups of water in a saucepan and bring to a boil. Mix 1 cup of full-fat soy flour to a paste with cold water. Beat 1 minute with manual egg beater and dribble into boiling water. Cook 5 minutes, then add juice of 2 lemons. Set mixture aside to cool. Curds will develop. Strain these through a fine strainer or triple thickness of cheesecloth. Use "as is" where called for; where firmer curd is required, pressure cook at 10 lbs for 1 hour.

GRAINOLA I

Opening Note: Anoint your cooking pot with warm water or a light coating of oil before you begin, to prevent sticking.

Oatmeal, Wheat Cereals, Soy Grits, Rice Grits, Barley Grits.

Pre-salt one cup of boiling broth, milk or water and gradually, in a steady stream, stir in 1/2 cup of meal. Reduce to a simmer, cover tightly and cook 5 minutes. Stirring during simmering results in gumminess. Curb your impatience.

Millet, Cornmeal, Buckwheat Groats, Rice Cream, Bulgur (Cracked Wheat), Couscous, Brown Rice, Kasha (Cracked Buckwheat).

Pre-salt 1 cup of the above liquid and add, as above, 1/3 cup of grain (excepting rice cream, of which add only 3 Tbs). Cook as above for 15 minutes.

Whole-Wheat, Barley, Steel Cut Oats, Rye, Triticale, Wild Rice.

Pre-salt 1 cup of the above liquid and gradually add 1/3 to 1/2 cup of grain. Cook as above for 30 minutes.

GRAINOLA II
(Flaked)

Combine 1 cup whole-wheat flakes, 1 cup soy flakes, and 1 cup of either flaked rye or barley, flaked pinto beans or rice, or flaked corn. 1 tsp salt. Heat 6 cups of mild broth or plain water to a boil and stir in flakes. Bring to a second boil, then reduce heat to a bare simmer, cover tightly and simmer 45 minutes. Store in glass jars with tight screw caps, or Mason jars. Do not make up more than you will use in one week (or freeze the excess). Keep refrigerated at all times. After cooking, you may further fortify the cooked grains with 1/2, or more, cups of cooked brown rice or steamed bulgur, before storing.

SUPER GRAINOLA II

Combine 1/2 cup each: uncooked rye, oat, wheat, soy, pinto bean, corn, millet flakes and cook as above in 6 cups liquid. Combine with 1/2 cup each: cooked kasha (buckwheat groats), wild rice, bulgur, and barley. Follow storage instructions above.

Tips:
    1 cup raw millet or whole buckwheat = 4 cups cooked; 1 cup raw rice = 3 cups cooked.
    Grainola is creamier if grain and liquid are premixed then boiled together.
    Grainola is thicker if allowed to "set," off the burner, after cooking time has elapsed. Allow an additional 10 minutes in the covered pot.

Grainola is more nutritious if under-cooked. Long cooking at high temperatures destroys B vitamins and protein. Starch is completely digestible when cooked at temperatures well below the boiling point, old porridge lore notwithstanding.

The warm-up: Do not reheat Grainolas over direct heat. Spoon into a strainer and warm up over bubbling water in a covered pot.

SEEDMEAT I
Snappy

Combine 1/4 cup of each of four of these seeds: alfalfa, radish, fenugreek, lentil, mung, soy, sunflower in a large wide-mouthed jar, fill with 2-1/2 times as much water as seed and fasten a doubled-up swatch of muslin, cheesecloth or netting over the top. After six hours or overnight, pour off, rinse, return jar to its incubating place (an unused oven, a dark cupboard, or the like) and continue to rinse seeds and drain 2 or 3 times daily until sprouts appear and grow to the desired length (at least twice the length of the seed).

SEEDMEAT II
Grainy

Using the germinating technique above, soak 1/4 cup each: triticale grain, buckwheat groats, brown rice, rye or whole-wheat. Refrigerate after harvesting and use quickly. This is perishable meat too. Here, too, you may want to enlarge on your grain repertoire in time.

VEGEMEAT
All Purpose

I
Wash 2 to 4 cups dried beans in cold water, pick them over and discard imperfect ones. Cover with water (twice as much water as beans) and bring to a boil. Reduce heat to a barely perceptible simmer and cook until tender (this will take anywhere from 1 to 5 hours, with soybeans requiring the longer time because of their much higher protein content). Do not salt during cooking as this tends to harden protein and increase the cooking time.

When cooked, put into blender, 1 cup at a time, with coarsely chopped carrots, onions, parsley and garlic (2 Tbs each for each cup of beans). Puree and put away in a covered jar or dish. Use up in one week.

II
Wash 2 to 4 cups dried beans and cover with boiling water. Let stand for 2 hours, change water and cover with boiling water again. Refrigerate and let beans soak 6 hours or more (longer for soybeans). Drain well and put through food grinder with the vegetable combination mentioned above. Store as above and use where partially cooked bean puree is appropriate.

Note: 1 cup raw beans = 4 to 5 cups cooked.

BASIC VEGETARIAN GELATIN

Powdered agar-agar, which is sea-green, rich in iodine and numerous other essential minerals and trace elements, makes delicious aspics, gelatins and desserts. Like the animal-derived commercial gelatin, it is low in calories.

1. Soak 1/4 oz agar-agar in 1 cup of cold water and soak until it is transparent. Drain off this water and pour on 2-1/2 cups boiling water (if planning to serve gelatin unmolded — otherwise use 3 cups).

2. Let agar-agar boil until thoroughly dissolved. Strain and add any fruit

30

juice desired as a flavoring, or any vegetable broth. When jelly begins to set, add chopped fruits or vegetables.

BUM STOCK 1
For Mock-Fish Dishes

Put 1 piece of stewing seaweed (wakame or kombu — if the former, soak first, then snip into 1/2'' pieces) into deep kettle with 1 tsp miso and 5 cups of plain water, or water left from boiling rice or noodles. Bring to a boil, then simmer at least 1 hour. Remove from heat, add 2 eggshells, bring to a second boil and cook 30 minutes longer (to clarify). Put 1 cup of stock in blender (yes, you have removed shells and any other extraneous matter) with 1 tsp gelatin which has been pre-mixed in 2 Tbs cold water, blend for 1 minute and return to stockpot. Gradually re-heat, slowly bringing to a final boil. Stir continuously till stock thickens somewhat. When cooled, add Vegebutcher salt, pepper and mushroom powder (optional) to taste, pour into jar, or refrigerate some and freeze the rest.

INSTANT BUM STOCK I

Use 1 cup of toasted and torn nori and/or dulse in place of stewing seaweeds. Reduce first cooking time to 30 minutes. Proceed as above.

> A virus found in most chickens is a possible cause of cancer in humans, reports Dr. Jack G. Markari at the annual meeting of the American Public Health Association.
> — reported in *Let's Live*, Jan., 1974

BUM STOCK II
For Mock-Meat Dishes

2 cups of seeds for toasting
1 cup of throwaway vegetables and crushed eggshells
1 Tbs miso
1 Tbs food yeast
2 Tbs seed oil
fresh garlic, fresh greens
toasted bean flour, 1-2 Tbs
6 cups of hot water or mushroom bouillon and 1 tsp lemon juice or vinegar
Vegebutcher salt to taste

1. Toasting seeds: 1 cup of small seeds in the dill-caraway-celery seed family are best combined with 1 cup of big seeds in the squash-pumpkin family. Avoid heady stuff like pomegranate and anise. When lightly toasted, pulverize in the blender.

2. Gather throwaway vegetables such as corn cobs (broken up), pea pods, carrot scrapings, broccoli bottoms and so on. Exclude beets and cabbage. Add crushed eggshells (for calcium). Chop all into manageable pieces.

3. Heat oil in bottom of a canner or large deep stockpot and saute garlic and greens (parsley, chives, celery leaves are all fine), which have been cut down to size.

4. Saute seedmeats very, very briefly, then stir in yeast and flour (soy, lima, or chick-pea will add nice flavor).

5. Add hot water and miso, lemon juice and throw away vegs, and eggshells and bring the pot to a full boil. Lower heat and simmer for 1-2 hours, covered.

6. Strain stock, add Vegebutcher salt to taste and decant into screw-top glass jars. Refrigerate.

INSTANT BUM STOCK II

In blender jar put 3 cups of hot water, 2 Tbs Vegebutcher salt, 1 tsp each garlic flakes and onion flakes, 2 Tbs peanut or sesame butter, 1 Tbs miso or soy sauce, 2

Tbs peanut or sesame oil, 1 tsp food yeast, 1 Tbs soy granules or oven-toasted soy flour. Blend thoroughly and store as above.

Note: Stock held more than a few days in the refrigerator should be heated to a boil before being used.

BOUILLON CUBES

Pour stock, not for immediate use, into small ice cube trays. When frozen, transfer to a plastic bag for one-at-a-time use in soups, stews, sauces, so on.

GRAVY MAKERS
Insta-Steer I: Starter-concentrate for Mock-Fish Gravies, Sauces, Etc.

In a heavy iron skillet or very heavy-bottomed deep pot put 4 cups of fresh Bumstock I and bring to a fierce boil. Let stock boil rapidly until it is reduced to about 1/4 cup or until brown and syrupy. Add 1 tsp miso or 1/2 tsp soy sauce. Store in a small jar and keep refrigerated. Use as specified. For additional flavor and smoothness, add 1 tsp wheat germ oil.

Insta-Steer II: Starter-concentrate for Mock-Meat Gravies, Sauces, Etc.

Follow the above directions using Bumstock II instead. If desired, a tsp of sesame oil may be added for extra flavor and smoothness when cooked.

Insta-Steer Savory: A Meaty-flavored Vegebutcher Roux.

Put 1/2 cup tomato juice, 1/2 cup soy sauce and 1 tsp Vegebutcher Salt in a   33 saucepan and bring to a boil. Remove pot from heat and pour the works into blender container, adding 1/4 cup brewer's yeast. When completely blended, gradually add an additional 3/4 cup of yeast. Additional contributions: fresh pressed garlic, 1 or 2 cloves, fresh grated onion, or shallot flakes.

Insta-Steer Onion/Garlic Basting Juice:

Combine half a large chopped onion and/or one small peeled head of garlic with one cup of water (more if you're using the garlic too) and blender-liquefy. Refrigerate for use in basting or to replace stock or broth required in any recipe.

MARINADES
The Marinade Base

1 Tbs freshly squeezed lemon br lime juice, 1/4 cup olive or other vegetable oil, 1 Tbs soy sauce and 1 Tbs Insta-Steer Savory, plus 1/4 cup Bumstock I (for fish) or II (for meats) or 1/4 cup vegetable broth or diluted tomato juice.

Mock-Chicken Marinade

To marinade base add: 1/2 tsp marjoram, 1 tsp chives, 1/2 tsp chervil or basil. Or you may simply add 1 Tbs poultry seasoning, good commercial version, or homemade (recipe later).

Mock-Beef and Game Marinade

To marinade base add: 1/2 tsp dried dill, 1/2 bay leaf or 1/4 tsp powdered laurel, 1/2 tsp thyme or fines herbes seasoning.

Mock-Pork Marinade

34 To the base add: 1/2 tsp each dried sage, caraway, savory or basil.

Mock-Lamb Marinade

To the base add: 1/2 tsp basil, 1/2 tsp rosemary, and 1/4 tsp peppermint or spearmint leaves.

Mock-Veal Marinade

To base add: 1/2 tsp tarragon, 1/2 tsp oregano, 1/4 tsp dried lemon peel.

Mock-Fish Marinade

To base add: 1/2 tsp tarragon, 1/2 tsp fines herbes seasoning or savory, 1/4 tsp turmeric, 1/4 tsp dried lemon peel.

Mock-Innards Marinade

To base add: 1/4 tsp powdered bay leaf, 1/2 tsp dill, 1/4 tsp mace or nutmeg.

Note: Measurements are for dried herbs, unless otherwise noted. When using fresh herbs, double the amount.

> "Gigantic quantities of corn and other grain are used up producing the juicy marbling — the flecks of saturated fat — which American consumers have come to like. "Prime" beef has the most saturated fat, as well as the most calories and the least amount of protein"
>
> — *New York Times* Magazine, Nov. 24, 1974

VEGEBUTCHER SALT

parsley flakes
onion flakes
garlic flakes*
bell pepper flakes
cumin seed*
celery seed
kelp powder
sea salt
black pepppercorns*
assorted dehydrated garden vegetable flakes
brewer's (or any nutritional) yeast flakes*

Put 1 tsp of all the starred* ingredients into your seed mill or blender and pulverize. Pour into a cup and blend 1/2 tsp of the remaining ingredients to a pulver. Combine the two powdered blends and decant (via a small funnel) into empty spice/herb jars.

Note: Make in small quantities and re-formulate when necessary.

VEGEBUTCHER SUPER-SALT

Proceed as above, but before decanting pulverize and add any or all of the following in 1/2 tsp quantities. Since Super-Salt is simply a "luxe" version of Vegebutcher Salt, there is no reason why you cannot (where you see fit) use it in place of its more basic brother.

mushrooms, dried
toasted squash or pumpkin seed
toasted black or white sesame seed
watercress (sold already dried)
briefly toasted poppy, dill or caraway seed

MOCK MSG

I

Grate 1 Tbs each: fresh lemon peel and fresh ginger-root. Dry at room temperature or in a very low oven until almost brittle. Grind with 1 tsp coarse salt in a seed grinder or with mortar and pestle until quite fine. Store in small well-capped vials or bottles. Use in pinches.

II

Grate 1 Tbs fresh horseradish root and dry in a warm kitchen overnight. When moisture is completely gone, pulverize with 1 Tbs dried mushrooms and 1 tsp whole mustard seed. Stir this powder into 2 tsps sea salt and store in well-capped spice jars.

Note: Commercially sold horseradish powder may be substituted. The quantity of powder used should be twice that of the fresh root.

BUM CRUMBS
All-purpose Breading Mix

1/2 cup whole-wheat bread or semi-sweet cake crumbs
1/4 cup non-instant milk powder
2 Tbs soy flour
paprika
2 Tbs toasted wheat germ or coarse bran
1 tsp Vegebutcher salt
1 tsp onion powder (optional)
1 tsp garlic powder (optional)

Combine everything in a small mixing bowl and put in small shaker jars. Keep one on refrigerator door and freeze the second for later.

HOMEMADE POULTRY SEASONING
A Super Salt for Pseudo-Fowl

8 parts sea salt (preferably large-crystal crude salt)
2 parts white or black peppercorns
2 parts dried sage
1 part each dried marjoram, savory and thyme
1/4 part dried rosemary
4 parts dried parsley
1 part powdered mace (optional)
part dried and finely ground lemon peel (or tangerine, grapefruit or lime peel)

Grind salt and pepper and peel just before blending. Combine with crushed parts of everything else. Put into shaker jars or emptied pill bottles with snap-caps. Stays fresh, if properly capped, for 6 months.

HOMEMADE PICKLING-SPICE MIX
For Soups, Sauces, Piquant Gravies

I
2 Tbs allspice, whole
2 Tbs black pepper, whole
2 Tbs mustard seed, whole
2 Tbs celery seed
2 Tbs dillweed

Combine in 2 muslin bags (large enough to allow pickling liquid to flow through) and fasten with butchers twine, clean kitchen string or length of dental floss. Store on pantry shelf in tea canister until needed. You may re-use each bag at least once.

II
1 bay leaf, whole
2 Tbs cardamom

2 cloves, whole
1 slice ginger-root
1 cinnamon stick
1 small dry chili pepper

Store in bags as suggested above.

Note: Coriander seed, mace, dill seed, caraway seed, star anise, and vanilla bean may also be used in compatible pickling-spice combinations of your own invention.

THE HERBIVORE'S HERBED POT
A Recipe

Meatless cooking is enhanced some when performed in pre-seasoned pots. If you have pottery pots, bag up a combination of your favorite potherbs (fresh or dried) in a muslin sack, put in the pot, fill 2/3 full of water, bring to a boil, reduce to a simmer and cook covered for an hour, after which, discard sack and water. Your pot is now herbally impregnated and ready to receive its first boulette, rillette, or ragout.

You may run through this same operation using a spice bag instead of herbs if you often use a pottery pot for fruit soups, jam, jelly, fruit-sauce-making, pear-poaching, etc.

MOCK MILK I

Combine 1 lb of soy flour with 3 quarts of cold water. Mix well and boil for 25 minutes, strain or press out milk with a ricer, sweeten and salt to taste.

MOCK MILK II

Grind 1 cup of raw cashews or almonds (or a mixture of both) in blender, gradually adding 2 cups of water and 2 Tbs honey. When completely blended, store and use as specified as a dairy milk substitute.

MOCK (SOY) BUTTER

Mix together 1/2 pint water and 2 Tbs soy flour. Put into a heavy skillet and boil 5 mins or until thickened. Strain into a mixing bowl. Pour in 1 pint of good minimally-processed soybean oil very slowly, as in preparing mayonnaise, beat constantly until proper consistency is reached. Store in refrigerator.

MOCK CREAM

Put 1 heaping Tbs soy flour and 1/2 cup water in a saucepan, combine thoroughly and heat, stirring constantly till thickened (five minutes of boiling is helpful). Strain or sieve and put juice in a mixing bowl. Slowly, beat in 1/2 cup soybean oil, adding it drop by drop so that it can be incorporated into the soy milk till a creamy consistency is reached. More oil will turn out a thicker cream. Sesame oil may be substituted for the soy oil or may replace part of it.

MOCK YOGURT

2-1/2 cups warm water
2 cups raw cashew nuts
3 Tbs honey
1/4 cup soy yogurt culture (see STEERAGE)

Blend everything till very smooth, pour into pre-warmed yogurt cups or dishes and incubate till properly cultured 3 or more hours (end product will be thinner than dairy counterparts), or until consistency and taste meets with your approval. Refrigerate.

Consumer beware! According to an Oct. 12, '74 report in the *New York Times*, "To produce meat-like fibers from the defatted soybean flour, first the carbohydrates are removed and the remaining solution of pure protein is pumped through a spinerette — a showerhead-like device with microscopic holes. As the protein emerges from the holes, it hits an acid bath that precipitates the protein as individual fibrils, which are neutralized and washed. The resulting tasteless, odorless, off-white fibers are then mixed with flavorings, coloring, fat, water and egg albumen, which acts as a binder. A cooking process coagulates the mass into slabs three-eighths of an inch thick . . ."

BOGUS BEEF

MOO-LESS RAGOUT
A Super Steamer Stew Inspired by China's Famous "Turn-out" Dishes

1/4 lb broccoli
1/4 lb cauliflower
2 Tbs soy butter or dairy butter
4 oz of Chinese cellophane noodles or extra-thin vermicelli
6 large Chinese dried mushrooms or 3 oz button mushrooms
2 Tbs soy sauce
2 zucchini
1 medium-sized eggplant
1 cup Tofu
oil for deep frying
1/2 tsp sea salt or Vegebutcher salt
1 Tbs cottage cheese
2 Tbs dry cider or sherry
1 cup Bumstock I, or Bumstock II (consider whether you have your mouth set for a fishy or meaty Ragout)

1. Grease the inside of a large heat-proof bowl with butter or oil.
2. Break cauliflower and broccoli into branches and flowerets and press against sides of bowl. Soak noodles in warm water for 5 mins. Drain, then mix with mushrooms (if dried were used, soak for 30 mins then gently squeeze dry) and pour into bowl.
3. Over this sprinkle 2 Tbs soy sauce.
4. Slice zucchini and eggplant into 1/2" thick slices, and Tofu into 8 slices. Place these in wire basket and deep-fry together for 3 mins.
5. Drain and place atop noodles. Sprinkle contents with salt, cider, and finally pour in stock.
6. Fasten a sheet of foil over top of bowl, place bowl in a large steamer (or set in a skillet filled with boiling water and tent with a large sheet of heavy-duty

43

foil; watch water carefully and refill with new boiling water as necessary) and steam steadily for 1 hour. By this time the liquid will be completely absorbed by the noodles.

7. Remove foil. Turn out Ragout onto a well-heated platter or casserole with deep sides. Serves 6 handily, meatily.

Suggested garnishes: a ring of raw Chinese long-beans, a nest of Chinese parsley (coriander), branches of fresh tarragon or dill.

BUM STEW I

2 cups prepared Gluten, cubed and presoaked in mock-beef marinade.
paprika, wheat germ, milk powder, Vegebutcher salt.
2 Tbs vegetable oil
1 cup cooked macaroni or sesame spirals pasta.

FOR SAUCE
2 Tbs oil
1 Tbs Vegebutcher salt
1 tsp nutritional yeast
1 tsp flour
1/2 tsp dry sage
1 tsp soy sauce
1 tsp lecithin granules
salt and pepper to taste
1 tsp onion flakes
1/4 cup dry mushrooms
1/4 cup any sprouted beans
raw cream and water as needed

1. Dredge Gluten chunks in paprika-wheat germ mix and let rest until coating hardens (20 or more minutes).
2. Heat vegetable oil in a skillet large enough to accommodate all stew pieces. Add chunks and place skillet in moderate oven (350°) until pieces are browned — about 40 minutes (you may turn them once after 20 minutes). Set oven-fried Gluten aside while you prepare sauce.

SAUCE:
1. Heat oil and stir in yeast, soy flour, broth powder. Stir until you have a smooth roux (take care not to burn — soy flour blackens more rapidly than wheat flours). Add 1/2 cup raw cream (or sour cream) and reduce heat. Cook, stirring constantly, until thickened.

2. Add remaining ingredients except for sprouts and pasta. Add as much water (or thin milk, if preferred) as necessary to make a good gravy. Stir in cooked pasta.

3. Adjust seasoning and put gravy and Gluten chunks into a serving casserole. Serve herbed bottled greens on the side.

BUM STEW II
Cowless Crock-Pot Cookery

FOR STEW
NOTE: best cooked in an electric crock pot, or a Dutch oven with an asbestos pad or flame-tamer over the burner to allow for slow, smug simmering.

1/2 cup olive oil
3 cups Bumstock II or vegetable broth
1 sliced celery root or 4 jerusalem artichokes or 1 peeled sliced black radish (worth a trip to your nearby farmer's market for whichever you can root out)
finely peeled and sliced turnip, taro root, parsnip or carrot
2 potatoes thinly sliced
2 leeks or 2 stewing onions, sliced or twice quartered
First option: 1/2 to 1 cup soaked lentils or chick-peas
Second option: 1 cup lightly cooked barley, noodles or rice
1 bay leaf, 1 tsp marjoram leaves, 1 tsp Vegebutcher salt

FOR STEWING:
1. Pour stock and oil into cooker.
2. Add vegetables in layers in the order above.
3. Bring stew to a boil. Turn heat down and let simmer 30 minutes, tightly covered, or longer in your crock-pot cooker.
4. Before finished, saute some scissored parsley or lightly chopped sprouts in 2 Tbs clarified butter and add to stew.

MEATBALLS
1 cup sifted whole-wheat flour
1/2 cup Seedmeat coarsely chopped
1 egg, separated
milk or Mock Milk
1 Tbs Vegebutcher salt

    1. Sift flour
    2. Whip egg white with beater until nearly stiff.
    3. Add milk and yolk as needed to make a thickish dough.
    4. Add salt and Seedmeat sprouts.
    5. Form into small balls the size of walnuts and drop into a kettle of boiling water. (They will double in size during cooking.)
    6. Simmer in covered kettle about 6 mins.
    7. Remove with slotted spoon and add to stew below.

STEW
    1. Combine 1/2 cup Bumstock or vegetable broth with 1 Tbs of Gravy Maker, and 1-1/2 cups Seedmeat and heat in a stew-pot over low heat for 15 mins.
    2. Transfer to blender and process till smooth.
    3. Add 1/2 cup crisp lentil sprouts (and warmed dairy or soy milk if sauce needs thinning) and the meatballs above.
    4. Sprinkle with Chinese salted black beans or lightly toasted poppy seeds.
    5. Serve with a side platter of Bum Wraps I (see MOCKING UP). (You can slice them into ribbons and spoon stew atop.)

PEPPER POT
A Beef-Less Red Bell Pepper Stew

3 cups chopped and seeded red bell peppers
1/3 cup olive oil
1-1/2 tsp each: minced garlic, coarse salt, ground fennel
a few crushed saffron threads
1/4 tsp sugar
1-1/2 cups dry white wine or half-and-half mixture of sparkling mineral
　　　water and cider
2 Tbs flour
1 cup water
1 cup each cubed cooked eggplant, cubed prepared Gluten, cubed prepared
Tofu (or 3 cups of any one)

　　1. Saute peppers in oil over moderate heat until softened (about 10 to 15 minutes).
　　2. Grind the spices in a seed mill or crush with a mortar and pestle. Add to peppers and cook for 2 minutes, stirring.
　　3. Add wine (or cider) and water. Increase heat to moderate-high, and cook, stirring for an additional 2 minutes.
　　4. Reduce heat and gradually sprinkle in flour.
　　5. Simmer over low heat for 10 minutes, stirring frequently.
　　6. Add the 3 cups Mock-Meat (Gluten, Tofu, eggplant) and simmer over low heat for 5 minutes. Taste, correct seasoning, and serve with Small Fry (see ON THE SIDE).

> "... Twice as much energy is required to produce a pound of fat as is needed to make a pound of lean red meat. In 1973 some 2.5 billion pounds of excess fat were trimmed from beef carcasses at the retail level, most of these trimmings represented wasted grain ..."
> — William E. Barksdale, President of the American Forage and Grassland Council. reported in the *New York Times*, Jan. 2, 1975

47

"MEAT": 2 cups prepared cubed Gluten
BREADING: 1/4 cup raw peanut meal and 5 Tbs dry milk powder plus 1 tsp
    ground turmeric
MOCK-BEEF MARINADE: 1/2 cup

1. Put cubed Gluten in marinade and let soak several hours or overnight, turning occasionally.
2. Drain "meat" and coat in breading. Secure about 4 cubes on metal or wooden skewers and let coating set (about 20 mins).
3. Grill over hot coals inside (a hibachi is nice hardware here) or outdoors on a grill, watching carefully (ground nuts burn readily), or bake in a moderate oven about 20 mins, turning once.

SAUCE
1. Combine leftover marinade with 1/2 cup peanut butter (raw and undoctored is best), 1 Tbs arrowroot starch, 1/4 cup water, a handful of fermented black beans if you have any, some coriander leaves if you have any, and blend thoroughly (by machine).
2. Heat, stirring all the while, til you have a medium-thick sauce.
3. Serve hot as a dip. Leftovers may be frozen in the sauce and served as a future freezer-stew for onc.

"The industrial world's way of eating is an extremely inefficient use of resources. For every pound of beef consumed, a steer has gobbled up 20 lbs. of grain. The same amount of food that is feeding 210 million Americans would feed 1.5 billion Chinese on an average Chinese diet."
— Jean Mayer, *Time* Magazine, Nov. 11, 1974

SHORT RIBS
Braised Celery in a Countrified Risotto

4 Tbs butter (dairy or soy)
1-1/2 cups chopped onion, shallot, and/or scallion (whatever the budget
    permits)
1/2 lb chopped mushrooms
1 bunch fresh celery, well washed and cut into "short ribs"
3 cups cooked brown rice
1 cup raw cashews or walnuts, chopped
1/3 cup snipped fresh dill weed
1/4 cup chopped parsley
1 tsp sea salt and 2 tsp Vegebutcher salt
freshly ground black pepper to taste
1/4 cup oil or butter
1 cup finely chopped onion
2 Tbs flour
vegetable broth or Bumstock II
2 cups plain yogurt, (or sour cream) room temp
2 eggs
1 Tbs snipped fresh dill weed and freshly ground black pepper for topping.

    1. Melt butter in a wok, dutch oven or stew-pot. Cook onions until tender but not browned. Add mushrooms and celery and cook over high heat, stir-frying, til liquid has evaporated.
    2. Stir in rice, nuts, dill, parsley, salt, pepper and eggs. Mix well and taste for seasoning.
    3. Melt the 1/4 cup oil in a separate saucepan or skillet and cook onion very slowly until brown and tender (about 15 mins). Sprinkle with flour, stir in yogurt or cream and bring to a high simmer, stirring.
    4. Add stock gradually until a smooth sauce is achieved. Thin to desired consistency.
    5. Add sauce to braised rib mixture and top with dill and pepper.

PIE FILLING
6 cups vegetable bouillon
1 diced onion
2 large fresh beefsteak tomatoes
2 cups cooked kidney beans
2 large scraped carrots cut into julienne strips
3 Tbs flour
2 diced ribs of celery
3 Tbs vegetable oil
1/2 tsp crumbled sage
1 Tbs chopped parsley
freshly ground pepper to taste
Vegebutcher salt

VEGETARIAN PIE CRUST
1 cup sifted vegetable flour (soy flour, chick-pea flour, etc.)
1/2 tsp each salt, sugar
1/2 cup cold mashed potatoes
6 Tbs vegetable oil

FILLING
   1. Heat the bouillon to boiling and add onion, celery, carrot. Cook til half done.
   2. Brown flour in a heavy skillet but don't let burn. Blend in vegetable oil and one cup of liquid from vegetables.
   3. Stir mixture until it is smooth. Add to vegetable mixture.
   4. Add kidney beans and seasonings.
   5. Grease a casserole dish and turn half of the vegetable mix into this, alternating with layers of sliced beefsteak tomato.
   6. Top with pastry crust (recipe follows), make a steam hole, and bake 10 minutes, at 400°. Reduce heat to 350° and bake 30 minutes longer or until pastry is nicely browned.

CRUST
1. Sift flour with sugar and salt and blend in potatoes with a fork until mealy.
2. Add vegetable oil and cut in with a pastry blender until mixture is broken into small crumbs.
3. Form pastry into a ball, put in plastic bag and chill at least 30 minutes.
4. Roll out on lightly floured board to about 1/8'' thickness and proceed as above.

FRUIT ESTOUFFADE FOR SIX
Meaty, Fruity Ragout

1 qt (4 cups) home-canned tomatoes
3 slices dried pineapple in 1'' chunks
2 slices dried papaya in 1'' chunks
1/3 cup dried apricots, cut up
2 cups lentils
4 cups Bumstock II
1 large onion and 2 garlic cloves minced
1/2 to 1 cup Tofu cut in strips
2 Tbs olive oil
3 tsp sea salt
pinch of Mock MSG

1. Simmer tomatoes and fruits together for 45 mins or until thickened.
2. In a separate pot, put lentils in Bum Stock and bring to a boil. Cover pot and simmer for 20 mins or until tender.
3. Heat olive oil in a skillet and saute onions and garlic, stirring until they are soft.
4. Add tomato mixture, onion mixture, salt and Mock MSG to lentils and stir to mix well. Stir in Tofu and simmer 10 mins to blend flavors.

Serve with Grainola I if it's wintertime. Serve with Grainola II if it's summer. And for any other season, ask yourself what George Bernard Shaw would have served in your place and you may have the answer. Anyway, don't leave out the lentils. Lentils are a mineral-rich and highly concentrated food. The soybean excepted, they are considered the most nourishing of all the legumes, and their protein is probably equal to that of the muscle meats in biological value.

VEGETARIAN ROLLADEN

1-1/2 lb eggplant
salt and 2 cups olive oil
fresh ground pepper
1-1/2 tsp crushed oregano
2 cups sprout tomato sauce (see THE MOCK CROCK)
1/2 lb mozzarella cheese
1/2 lb cooked ground soybeans
1/2 cup chopped onion
1 finely chopped clove garlic
2 Tbs finely chopped parsley
1/2 cup grated parmesan cheese

1. Trim ends of eggplant and cut into very thin slices (you should have about 20 of them). Sprinkle both sides lightly with salt and place on rack. Drain 1 hour. Pat dry.
2. Heat 2 cups oil in large skillet and when almost smoking, add sliced eggplant, turn once and cook quickly. Drain.
3. Saute onion, garlic and ground soybean with pepper and oregano. After five minutes add parsley.
4. Lay slices of eggplant on flat surface and place a spoonful of filling in the center of each.
5. Spoon a thin layer of sauce over bottom of baking dish. Roll up eggplant slices to enclose filling and arrange rolls in one layer over bottom of dish. Add a layer of sauce. Arrange slices of mozzarella over the rolladen and cover with remaining sauce. Sprinkle with additional oregano and parmesan cheese. Bake 30 mins at 400° til casserole is hot and bubbly. 4 to 6 servings.

GOOD RED MEAT
Inspired by the Chinese Red-Stewed Meats

2 cups prepared Gluten or Tofu cut in cubes
3 Tbs peanut or other vegetable oil
1 whole scallion, chopped
2 thin slices peeled fresh ginger root
1 clove garlic, crushed
1/4 cup medium-dry sherry or apple cider
1/2 cup soy sauce
2 tsp brown sugar
2 cups Bumstock II

1. Heat oil in a wok or wide-mouthed skillet and when hot, brown cubed Gluten or Tofu. Brown on all sides, and add scallion, ginger and garlic. Stir-fry this mixture (adding more oil if necessary) until scallion is lightly browned.
2. Transfer mixture to a deep heavy pan and add soy sauce.
3. Cook over moderate heat for 1 min. Add sherry or cider and sugar. Bring to a simmer. Add broth, heated, and bring to a boil over high heat.
4. Reduce heat to a mere simmer and cook covered for 1 hour.

Serve with Shaken Peas (see ON THE SIDE) plus some additional steamed snow peas.

SALISBURY FAKE-STEAK
North Indian Style

FOR FILLING
1. Soak 2/3 cup golden raisins in a bowl of hot water for 2 hours.
2. Drain, chop and combine with 2 Tbs minced mint leaves.

FOR PATTIES
1. In large mixing bowl, combine 2 cups Vegemeat with 2 garlic cloves, 1 tsp Vegebutcher or poultry seasoning salt, 1/8 tsp pepper. Put through food grinder

with 1 large thick slice of day-old bread. Moisten slightly with broth or melted butter and knead with hands on a smooth surface for 5 minutes.

2. Divide mixture into 5 patties and tuck about 1 tsp raisin mixture into the center of each patty. Lift edges to enclose filling and roll each into a firm, smooth fat steak.

3. In a heavy skillet, heat 1/2 cup vegetable oil over moderately high heat and add 4 cardamom pods, crushed and tied in muslin bag. Stir-fry for 2-3 seconds, then add the steaks to brown (you may want to pre-bread the steaks with corn-starch or arrowroot for a crispier crust) on both sides. Transfer to a heated dish and reserve oil. Remove cardamom bag and reserve.

4. In a blender, process 6 garlic cloves, peeled and crushed with 1/3 cup water, a 1″ piece of peeled fresh ginger root, 1 Tbs grated coconut, 1/2 tsp pepper, 1/4 tsp mace and the cooked cardamom until it is pasty.

5. In reserved oil, saute 3 chopped onions until golden. Reduce heat to low, add garlic paste and cook for 1 minute. Blend in 1/2 cup thick tomato paste, 1/2 cup plain yogurt, and return cooked cardamom. Stir well and simmer gently, covered, for 30 minutes.

6. Remove cardamom bag, correct seasoning, and pour sauce over steaks arranged in an oval skillet (or if you've got a pre-seasoned flower-pot saucer of generous dimensions, here's a good place to use it. Directions for preparing saucer in THE MOCK CROCK).

7. Serve garnished with mint sprigs, ginger-root flowers (if you raise your own ginger plants) or kumquats with leaves on, on a bed of buttered 100% Vegetarian Noodles (see ON THE SIDE), unless you have a better idea.

MEATLESS MEATBALLS

1 cup of Vegemeat I made with chick-peas (garbanzos)
1/2 cup whole millet seed, ground, or cornmeal
1 egg separated
1/2 carrot, 1/2 onion, 1/2 stalk celery
2 tsp Vegebutcher Salt
1 slice of homemade bread, maybe

1. Separate egg and whip white.

2. Grind chick-peas in blender or food mill along with vegetables.

3. Grind millet, then toast in a moderate oven, stirring once during the 15 min toasting time.

4. Combine yolk, ground beans, millet and seasoning. Fold in beaten white. Shape into small meatballs, using fingers. If mixture needs added bulk, pulverize bread slice and incorporate. Chill balls for 1 hour.

5. Put balls in greased steamer in saucepot and steam, tightly covered for 15 minutes.

Serve with "spaghetti" (see next recipe) and Sprout Tomato Sauce (see THE MOCK CROCK) or whatever other sauce the above puts you in the meatless mood for.

Spaghetti-less Spaghetti for Meatless Meatballs

SPAGHETTI I
Fork-whip 2 large eggs with 2 Tbs dairy or mock yogurt (or sour cream) and 1 Tbs Vegebutcher salt, and pour 1/4 cup at a time into a skillet where you've pre-heated (moderately high heat) 1 Tbs sesame oil. Egg batter should cover entire pan surface, as in crepe baking. When cooked, carefully loosen and cook briefly on reverse side. When the 4 pancakes are cooked and cooled enough to handle, cut into thin ribbons of spaghetti. Top with meatless meatballs and sauce.

SPAGHETTI II
Briefly steam 2 or more cups of long-grain freshly-raised sprouts (soy is best), do or don't toss with an extra 1/2 cup of alfalfa sprouts (not steamed), and serve as above.

> ". . . traditional American reliance on meat, particularly beef, is perhaps the single largest inefficiency in world dietary patterns . . ."
> — *New York Times* Oct. 25, 1974

1 lb fresh mushrooms
1/2 cup minced onion and 4 shallots
3 Tbs butter and 1 Tbs oil
4 phyllo leaves (for strudel pastry)
1/2 cup sour cream
2 Tbs minced dill
salt, pepper
6 Tbs butter or vegetarian butter (soy oleomargarine)

1. Trim and mince mushrooms, put them in a tea towel, a handful at a time, and squeeze out moisture.
2. In a skillet saute mushrooms with onion and minced shallot with 3 Tbs butter and 1 Tbs oil until moisture has evaporated.
3. Stir in sour cream, dill, salt and pepper (to taste) and let mixture cool completely.
4. Have 4 phyllo leaves ready and 6 Tbs melted butter (or vegetarian butter). Put 1 leaf on a sheet of waxed paper, brush with butter and top with second leaf. Brush this with butter, keeping the remaining leaves covered with a damp tea towel.
5. Spread a 1'' wide strip of the mushroom filling along one of the long sides of the buttered phyllo. Fold in the sides of the leaves to contain the filling, and roll up the leaves jelly-roll fashion. Transfer the roll to a buttered baking sheet, seam side down, and make a second roll in the same manner. Brush the rolls with melted butter and bake them in a preheated moderate (350°) oven. Serve 4 with 100% Vegetarian Noodles II (see ON THE SIDE).

GREENWORKS GARNISH
Peel a fair-sized cucumber with a vegetable-paring tool to produce a single half-inch-wide spiral. Crisp til needed in icy salted water.

GREENBUTCHER'S MEATBALLS

1 large bunch fresh spinach (about 8 oz.)
2 cups Tofu, mashed
4 eggs, beaten
1/3 cup freshly grated parmesan cheese
1 cup Bum Crumbs or finely ground whole-wheat crumbs
2 tsp freshly minced basil (half that, i dried)
2 cloves garlic, crushed and chopped
1 Tbs fresh minced parsley
2 Tbs soy lecithin (optional)
salt and pepper to taste
pinch nutmeg
1 cup whole-wheat flour

1. Wash spinach well and put in a heavy pot with about 2 Tbs water. Cover and steam 5 mins. Greens should be just wilted.
2. Mince spinach finely and squeeze out as much liquid as possible.
3. Mix with remaining ingredients except flour. Add flour, in small amounts until mixture is fairly stiff. Shape small balls and chill 2-3 hours.
4. Bring water to a boil and add salt. Drop balls into boiling water and remove with slotted spoon when they rise to the top. Serve with Moo-less Meat Sauce (see THE MOCK CROCK).

HUTSPOT POT ROAST
A Potato Stew Inspired by the Meatless Dutch "Stamppotten" Dishes

2 large onions
4 Tbs mock or dairy butter and 2 Tbs oil
2 lbs (about 4 medium-sized) baking potatoes
1 lb carrots or parsnips cut into 1'' chunks
3 cups water or vegetable broth
1/3 cup milk
Vegebutcher salt to taste
1 Tbs Insta-Steer II
Raw peas (optional garnish)

1. Coarsely chop onions and combine with butter and oil.

2. Cook over medium-high heat, stirring occasionally until limp and golden, about 15 mins. Keep warm.

3. Peel potatoes (save peelings and see note below) and combine with carrots or parsnips in a saucepot with broth. Bring to a boil, lower heat and simmer covered for 20 mins until pieces are soft.

4. Drain (reserve liquid) and mash vegetables, with milk. Stir in onion mixture and add salt to taste, plus Insta-Steer starter.

5. Put into a well-oiled fluted flan pan or a flattish casserole (or even a well-washed, well-oiled flower pot saucer) and keep in a low oven til ready to serve with or without Potato Peelings Gravy (see THE MOCK CROCK). Garnish dish with a scattering of raw peas.

GOOBER BURGERS
With Goober Burger Sauce

BURGERS
1-1/2 cups ground roasted unsalted goobers (peanuts)
1 cup soft well-packed bread crumbs
1 beaten egg
1 Tbs mushroom powder
2 Tbs powdered parsley or watercress
1 tsp salt or kelp
3/4 cup plain yogurt

1. Mix all ingredients thoroughly. Chill 2 hours. Drop by heaping dessert-spoonfuls onto a hot greased skillet or griddle. Brown 5 mins each side (nuts burn easily).

2. Serve with Goober Burger Sauce (recipe follows), on hamburger buns.

SAUCE
1/4 cup minced onion
1/2 cup peanut butter
1/2 tsp salt

1 Tbs butter
1 cup bouillon or water
1 Tbs lemon juice
1/2 tsp crushed dried red pepper

1. Saute onion in butter until tender. Add bouillon or water and peanut butter. Stir until smooth.
2. Add remaining ingredients and serve hot.

ROLLED RUMP OF PEANUT

1 cup tomato puree
1 cup water or broth
2 Tbs gluten flour
1 cup ground toasted peanuts
1/2 tsp liquid pepper
2 Tbs powdered bell pepper flakes
1 tsp garlic powder
1/4 cup whole-wheat flour
1 cup soy grits
2 Tbs toasted wheat germ
2 Tbs soy sauce
1/4 cup finely chopped peanuts for texture
1/2 tsp garlic flakes

1. Put everything but 1/4 cup of peanuts in blender. Process, place in a bowl and fold in the omitted peanuts.
2. Grease 2 juice cans and fill 3/4 full. Cover with a patch of plain brown paper and secure with rubber bands or string.
3. Steam in a canner or deep kettle of simmering water for 2-3 hours until firm. (Cans should stand on a rack in water reaching about 2/3 of the way up the can.)
4. To remove from baking can: loosen around edges with table knife. Cool slightly before slicing.

TARTARE STEAKS
Heifer-free Beef-in-the-raw

I

1/2 lb mixture of cracked millet, corn, sunflower seeds (purchase at a grain-supplies store)
8 ounces peanut butter
salt, wild chives, garlic powder to taste

    1. Steam cracked grains until soft, about 1 hour.
    2. Mix with peanut butter and seasoning.
    3. Shape into generous tartare patties.
    4. Serve without cooking. Embellish with a raw fertile egg if you are honoring the custom.

II

1 cup soaked lentils
1 green onion
1 cup chopped celery
1 tsp hickory-smoked salt
1 cup fresh corn kernels
1/4 cup peanut butter
1 tsp Vegebutcher salt
1/2 tsp fresh cracked pepper

    1. Soak lentils in warm broth or Bumstock II overnight.
    2. Put corn, lentils, onion and celery through food grinder.
    3. Add remaining seasonings and mix thoroughly.
    4. Form into tartare patties. Serve uncooked, with the customary raw egg placed atop.

Mock Meatballs for the Eggetarian

I *(translated from the Chinese)*
4 large eggs with good shells (pullet eggs if you are a stickler for traditions)
1 tea bag (any type but green)
soy sauce
salt
star aniseed or cinnamon stock

    1. Boil the eggs, starting in cold water over medium heat. Ten mins after eggs start to boil, cool them in cold water.
    2. Make a broth by boiling tea bag in water for 5 mins and then add enough more water to cover the number of eggs you've cooked.
    3. For each cup of broth add 1 Tbs soy sauce, 1 tsp salt, 1 whole star aniseed.
    4 .Crack the hard-boiled eggs gently all over with the bottom of a spoon.
    5. Immerse eggs in broth, bring to a boil and simmer about 30 mins. Let stand overnight. Peel, cut into wedges and serve cold with a simple soy sauce or a soy-spiked mock mayonnaise.

II *(inspired by the famous Tigers Eggs of Central China)*
4 large hard-boiled eggs
oil for deep frying
Bumstock I or II with additional soy sauce

    1. Shell eggs and place in cold oil in a high-sided cooking pot, and heat.
    2. When oil begins to boil, eggs will start to bubble. At this point, reduce heat and continue cooking til eggs are well fried.
    3. Remove eggs from oil and dump into cold water immediately.
    4. Fill a pan with Bumstock and some extra soy sauce and simmer eggs until seasoning gets into egg white (the longer you simmer, the saltier your "meatballs").

Serve with Chinese noodles, rice or stir-fried greens.

FAKE SWISS STEAK
Transcendental Vegetation

STEAK
1 large eggplant
1 bunch of fresh swiss chard
3 Tbs olive oil

SAUCE
1 Tbs minced capers
1 tsp miso or marmite
4 green onions minced
1 mashed clove garlic
1 Tbs each, minced basil and parsley
1 pinch rosemary
1 Tbs olive oil
2 tsp lemon juice
1 twist of minced lemon rind
salt to taste

1. Slice eggplant into 1-1/2'' thick "steaks", salt and let drain 1 hour. Then pat or gently squeeze dry.
2. Divide chard in half, cut off stems and save these for stock-making or as a side vegetable for another meal.
3. Quickly rinse leaves and steam very briefly until easy to handle.
4. Heat olive oil in large skillet or wok and brown steaks well on each side. (You may flavor the frying oil with a mashed clove of garlic if desired.)
5. When steaks and leaves are cool enough to handle, wrap each steak in a leaf and arrange on the bottom of a large casserole or ovenproof baking dish.
6. Put all ingredients for sauce in blender container and process. Heat briefly, pour over steaks and bake in a 350° oven for 45 mins.

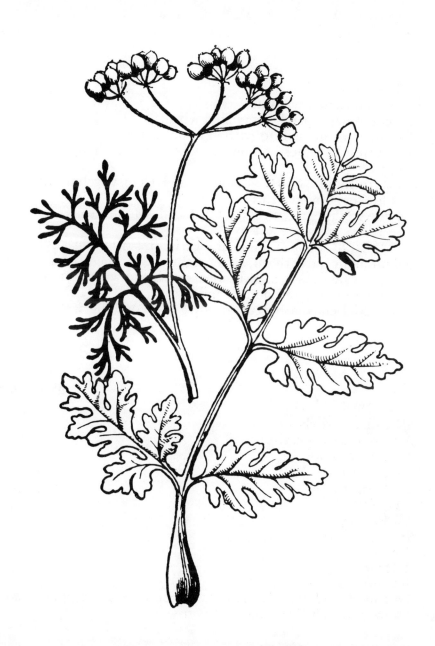

WHEAT LOAF

2 Tbs walnut oil
1/2 cup unsalted walnuts
1/2 cup bulgur (parched cracked wheat)
1/2 large organic potato with skin on, grated
4 Tbs freshly minced onion or scallion and 1 chopped garlic clove
1 egg
1 tsp, or more, poultry seasoning and 1 tsp Vegebutcher salt, pepper, 1/2 tsp
    hickory-smoked salt
1/4 cup freshly grated romano or parmesan cheese

1. Saute chopped onion and garlic in skillet with 2 Tbs walnut oil. Stir in bulgur and coat with oil, cover tightly. Steam-cook for 15 mins.
2. Grind nuts to a gritty meal and blend with beaten egg. Put in bowl with soy granules and seasonings and cheese.
3. Add cooked bulgur to bowl and combine well, using fingers. If more moisture is needed, add a bit of milk or broth. Bake 30 minutes at 325°.

MOCK MAC I
Macadamia Nut-Burgers

3/4 to 1 cup soybeans
3 pressed cloves garlic
1/8 tsp cayenne
1 tsp oregano
1 tsp paprika
1 tsp salt
1/2 tsp kelp
1/2 cup sherry
2 beaten eggs
2 Tbs milk
1/2 onion finely chopped
1/4 cup ground macadamia nuts (filberts are an acceptable substitute)
1/4 lb grated cheddar cheese if you want a cheeseburger

1. Crack or split beans in food mill. Soak overnight and cook in soaking water for 2 hours with ingredients from garlic to and including sherry.

2. Cool beans completely and mix the remaining ingredients except for cheese. (If not using small soybeans, you may want to chop the cooked beans slightly in blender.)

3. Spoon out large patties (about 5) into a greased baking pan or baking sheet and put into a 325° oven. Bake 10 minutes, sprinkle with grated cheese (you may omit this) and bake an additional 5 mins. Or brush with 1 Tbs soy sauce and broil for 3 mins.

MOCK MAC II
McIntosh Apple-Burgers

BURGER
1 cup shredded McIntosh apple (skin and all if unsprayed)
1 cup Grainola
1 large egg
1/2 tsp lemon peel, finely ground, 1/4 tsp freshly grated pepper, 1/2 tsp mace,
     1 tsp homemade poultry seasoning and 1 tsp Vegebutcher salt
1 Tbs walnut oil (or vegetable or sesame oil) for skillet
3 Tbs Bum Crumbs

1. Squeeze shredded apple until as dry as possible and put in mixing bowl with everything but last 3 ingredients.

2. Stir or combine well, using fingers, until everything is thoroughly mixed. (If still too moist for burgers, add toasted wheat germ or fine bread crumbs.)

3. Grease large skillet or griddle, form fat burgers with your hands, and dredge with Bum Crumbs.

4. Bake burgers til well browned, turn and brown bottoms. Set aside while making sauce.

SAUCE
2 cups apple cider
1 Tbs butter

1. Combine cider with 1 Tbs butter. Boil away in a pre-greased heavy-bottomed saucepan until thick and syrupy and reduced to about 1/4 cup.

2. Pour over waiting Mock Macs garnished with fresh chicory.

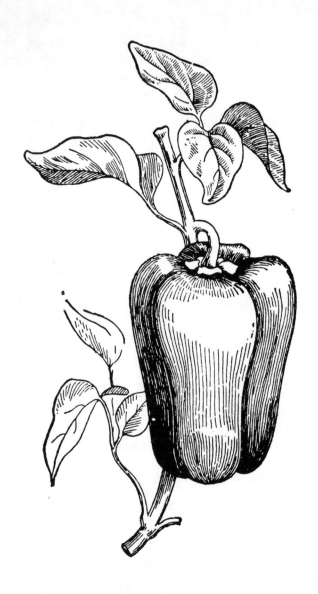

PSEUDO PORK

Like MSG, the nitrites which are in frankfurters, bacon, ham and salami, are a fre-
quent cause of migraine headaches.
— *American Family Physician*,
vol. 6, Dec., 1972

RED HOTS
Flesh-free Finger Franks

4 large red bell peppers
1/2 cup lightly packed fresh basil leaves, chopped
1/4 cup chopped parsley
3 Tbs olive oil
2 Tbs chopped walnuts
1 garlic clove, minced
1/4 tsp each pepper and coarse salt

1. Broil 4 bell peppers under preheated broiler 4 to 5 inches from the heat for 3 or 4 mins on each side and both ends or until skins are charred. While still warm, extract and discard stems. With sharp knife, peel off skins, halve peppers and scrape off seeds and ribs. Cut each pepper in thirds lengthwise.

2. Put remaining ingredients in blender and puree, stopping machine frequently to push herbs down into the blades with a spatula. Spread a thin layer of this filling on the inside of each pepper strip and roll up strips starting with narrow end. Secure rolls with wooden picks. When well secured, gently dislodge picks and stuff into warm hotdog buns and cover with a relish or a mock-meat mustard (see THE MOCK CROCK).

67

At-home Take-out Food from the Pecan Pork Barrel

PORK
1 cup shelled walnut or pecan halves

BATTER
1 beaten egg, 1/2 cup water or stock, and flour to make a moderately sticky
    batter.
oil for deep-frying.

SAUCE
1 mashed garlic clove
1 stalk of celery shredded on grater
1/2 bell pepper, grated or finely minced
2 Tbs tomato puree
2 Tbs soy sauce
1 cup Bum Stock or broth
1 Tbs cornstarch mixed with 3 Tbs cold stock or broth
3 slices ginger root
1 tsp sugar
1 tsp sesame oil

    1. Combine batter ingredients and heat oil to 300° for frying.
    2. Prepare "pork" pieces by toasting 15 minutes in a 220° oven.
    3. Dip nuts in batter and lift out with a small spoon, leaving only enough
batter on each nut to cover entirely. Scrape the bottom of the spoon on the rim of
the bowl before transferring the nuts to the oil. Turn nuts once for even frying.
Set aside and keep warm while you prepare sauce.

SAUCE
    1. Put 3 Tbs of oil in a wok or skillet. When hot, add garlic and ginger and
cook just 5 seconds.
    2. Add remaining ingredients and cook 5 mins at the boiling stage.
    3. Thicken with cornstarch. Stir til smooth and add fried nuts.
    4. Serve with Noodle Fry (see ON THE SIDE), and garnish with celery

leaves.

WONDER WIENER I

1 cup shredded carrots
2/3 cup finely chopped pinenuts (or peanuts for economy's sake)
2 well-beaten eggs
1/4 tsp powdered sage
1/2 tsp Vegebutcher salt
2 Tbs oil or melted butter
1/2 tsp powdered celery seed
2/3 cup Bum Crumbs toasted (or whole-wheat crumbs)

1. Add carrots and nuts to eggs and mix thoroughly.
2. Add sage, celery seed, salt, and butter. Blend in crumbs and nuts.
3. Lightly oil a cast-iron cornstick griddle (a less-successful substitute is a *madeleine* baking pan) and fill each cavity full.
4. Bake wieners in preheated 350° oven for 15 minutes until they are firm.
5. Dribble with a bit of oil and soy sauce and run under broiler briefly to brown tops.
6. Cool briefly and remove carefully using thin scraper or table knife. Eat out of hand.

WONDER WIENER II
With a Built-in Wrapper Bun Inspired by the Famous Lumpia of the Philippines

WRAPPER BUN
2 eggs
1/2 cup arrowroot or cornstarch
1/4 tsp salt
1-1/4 cups cold water
vegetable oil

Mix everything but water, then add water very slowly in a stream, whipping all the while (a whisk is the best tool here). Heat a 7 or 8'' skillet or crepe pan and brush lightly with oil. Spread a thin, even layer of batter in pan with a pastry

69

brush. Cook over moderately high heat until it blisters and is opaque. Gently loosen wrapper from pan with metal spatula and turn out onto a tea towel. Continue making wrapper buns until batter is used up.

WIENER FILLING *(best prepared in a wok or a sizable skillet)*
2 Tbs minced onion and 2 crushed garlic cloves
2 Tbs vegetable oil
1 cup Seedmeat
1 cup Grainola
1/2 cup Vegemeat (your choice)
1 finely grated sweet potato
1/2 cup medium-coarsely grated Chinese cabbage or savoy cabbage leaves
2 Tbs soy sauce
1/2 cup grated fresh green pepper
Vegebutcher salt

1. Saute onion and garlic in oil over moderately high heat, for one min.
2. Add raw vegetables, reduce heat and cover, cooking for 3 mins.
3. Uncover, add Seedmeat, Grainola, Vegemeat, soy sauce; stir-fry a few mins, season with salt to taste. Makes about 4 cups filling.

TO ASSEMBLE AND COOK
1. Put 2-3 Tbs filling on center of each wrapper, fold in edges, and roll wrapper to enclose filling.
2. Put 4 or 5 wieners, seam side down, in basket of a deep fryer. Heat 3″ of vegetable oil to 360° and very slowly lower basket into oil, allowing it to set the lower half of the wieners and prevent them from opening.
3. Fry for 2 mins until golden. Transfer with tongs to paper towels to dry. Fry remaining wieners in the same fashion. Makes about 20.

PIG-LESS PORK SAUSAGE

1 medium onion, chunked
1/2 lb diced mushrooms
1 cup Grainola, your choice

1 cup soaked and drained garbanzo beans or garbanzo bean sprouts
1/4 cup Mock-Pork Marinade
1/4 cup boiled milk
1 Tbs Insta-Steer Savory
2 cups prepared Gluten
1 Tbs chopped parsley
2 eggs
5 or 6 feet of sausage casing,* or lots of cheesecloth and string

    1. Put onion, mushrooms, Grainola, beans, and Gluten through your food grinder and then into a mixing bowl.
    2. Add marinade, beaten eggs, parsley, savory and milk.
    3. Combine well and let sit overnight to intensify flavors.
    4. Tie one end of the casing with string and fill from the other end (don't pack too snugly, because there will be some expansion during the cooking). Tie in 4-5" lengths.
    5. Place sausages in hot water kept just below boiling point. Cook 15 mins, remove, cool, refrigerate.
    6. To serve, broil 10 mins or bake in a hot oven about 20 mins. Pierce with fork before doing either.

Stuffing is best handled with the aid of a sausage stuffing horn or pastry bag. Serve with Breakfast Squares (see MOCKING UP).

CHEESECLOTH CASING
Wash and wring dry cheesecloth. Cut double thicknesses of the fabric 3" longer and 2" wider than the sausages you want and place cloth on a cookie sheet. Paint wrappings with vegetable (preferably olive) oil. Form sausages into rolls on cheesecloth covers and tie string around ends of, and middle of, your would-be weenies. Remove casing, after cooking and cooling, before eating.

---

* Sausage casing can be purchased in specialty stores or ethnic food stores, or see note in *Sending Away for Stuff* (STEERAGE).

2 small pineapples
3 Tbs salad oil
about 1-1/2 lbs Tofu I
1 clove minced garlic
1 small onion and 1 small green pepper thinly sliced
pig sauce (follows)
2 or more cups any Grainola

1. Halve pineapples, cutting through crown, with serrated knife. Cut fruit from rind leaving shell intact; reserve shells. Trim away cores, then cut fruit in 1/2'' thick chunks.

2. Pour 2 Tbs oil in wok or wide skillet, bring to a high heat and add garlic and cubed Tofu. Cook, stirring constantly for about 4 mins. Turn out of pan and add last Tbs oil. Add onion and pepper and cook 1 min. Add sauce, then pineapple. Cook until liquid boils and thickens. Return Tofu to pan and stir to combine.

3. Spoon Pig into pineapple boats and serve with bowls of steaming grain. Garnish with sprigs of watercress. Serve with Pickled Ears (see ON THE SIDE).

PIG SAUCE
Combine in blender: 1/4 cup honey and 1/4 cup cider vinegar, 2 Tbs chopped cress, 1 tsp Mock MSG I, 1 Tbs sherry and 1 Tbs soy sauce, 2 Tbs tomato sauce, pinch ginger and 1/4 cup vegetable broth. Heat in saucepan, stirring until thickened.

> "The protein you get in a frankfurter is expensive . . . an average of 81 cents a pound for all-meat samples and 92¢ for all beef franks. Those figures work out to average costs per pound of protein of $6.98 and $7.94 respectively. . ."
> — *Consumer Reports, 1972*

BRAISED SPARERIBS
Pork from the Garden Patch

3 heads of fresh fennel for about 18 spareribs (or celery as second choice)
4 Tbs butter or mock butter
3/4 cup Bumstock II or vegetable broth
1/2 tsp Mock MSG II (optional)
1 Tbs Insta-Steer I (or miso or marmite)
1 Tbs fresh lemon juice
1 tsp butter and 1 tsp flour
toasted millet (about 4 Tbs) for topping
grated dried lemon peel
salt and pepper

1. Trim fennel (or celery) and cut off any discolored leaves. Scrub well under running water. Cut each root in half and slice into "spareribs" and lay them in a single layer in a saute pan.

2. Cut butter in small pieces and scatter over "ribs."

3. Pour on stock, MSG, Insta-Steer, lemon juice, salt and pepper (to taste). Bring to a boil. Immediately lower heat and simmer gently for 1-1/2 hours, turning from time to time and adding more stock if needed.

4. Transfer to serving platter, thicken juices by stirring in butter and flour (mix them first to a paste). Stir til smooth and pour over "ribs." Sprinkle with oven-toasted millet seed and lemon peel. Serve with Smokehouse Vegetables (see ON THE SIDE).

> The quality of commercial pork in the United States is declining and is expected to get worse, according to three professors of meat science at Penn State University. Restricted or limited feeding regimens and faulty breed selection are at fault, they say.
> —*Organic Farming and Gardening*, Oct., 1974

GARDEN PATCH PORK IN A PAPER BAG
Pseudo Pork in a Warm-Up Suit (Stays Warm up to 2 Hours)

PORK
1/2 cup Mock-Pork Marinade
1 lb eggplant, peeled and cut into 1/4'' dice

SAUCE
2 Tbs minced onion and 1 garlic clove
1/4 cup butter or olive oil
1 Tbs minced parsley
1 tsp oregano
1 cup plain yogurt
reserved marinade juices
salt and pepper to taste
grated parmesan cheese

PASTA
1 lb cooked spaghetti or 1 lb homemade 100% Vegetarian Noodles (see ON THE SIDE)

PRE-COOKING
    1. Soak eggplant dice overnight in marinade
    2. Next day, squeeze pieces, then towel-dry. Set aside while you:
    3. Saute onion, garlic and herbs in butter.
    4. Add eggplant cubes and saute for 5 or 10 mins, or until tender.
    5. Stir in yogurt and marinade and set aside while preparing pasta.
    6. Combine pasta with "pork" and sauce and spoon into an insulated ice-cream bag. Insert bag into a second larger paper (foil preferred) bag and put in a 250-275° oven until you're ready to eat. Or take-along for outdoor or in-car eating. Serve with Pickled Heads (see ON THE SIDE).

GARDEN PATCH PORK LOIN
Sow-less Involtini

2 lbs spinach
1/4 cup minced onion
2 Tbs butter or oil
1/4 tsp nutmeg
2 lbs potatoes
Mock-Pork Marinade
2 cups whole-grain sifted flour
2 whole eggs and 1 egg yolk
pinch nutmeg and 1/4 tsp Vegebutcher salt and pepper or kelp
cheesecloth

    1. Cook 2 lbs of washed and trimmed spinach for about 5 mins in only the water that clings to the leaves. Drain and squeeze well, coarsely chop and transfer to a bowl. Stir in onion, lightly browned in the butter, plus salt, pepper and nutmeg. Let mixture cool.

    2. In a kettle, boil "pork" pieces (quartered potatoes) in enough marinade to cover (you may extend it with a little broth or milk) until tender. Drain, steam them dry for a few mins, then peel, put through a ricer or sieve and let cool.

    3. Stir in flour, and remaining ingredients and form dough into a ball (adding more flour if dough seems too sticky). Roll dough into a 13 x 11" rectangle on well-floured sheet of wax paper.

    4. Spread spinach mixture over dough, leaving 1" border on all sides, fold edges over filling and, beginning with one of the long sides, roll up the dough jelly-roll fashion, removing the paper while rolling.

    5. Press edges together well, wrap "loin" in cheesecloth and tie ends of cloth. Tie a 1-1/2" wide strip of cheesecloth around center of loin. Lower loin into a large oblong pan filled with enough boiling diluted marinade to cover and simmer for 1/2 hour.

    6. Carefully lift loin from pan and remove cloth.

    7. Carve loin into 3/4" slices and serve (to 6, 7, or 8) with Italian Green Sauce (see THE MOCK CROCK).

Results will be twice as porker-perfect with a garnish of tiny lady-apples (baked or raw) and sprigs or garlands of fresh sage or marjoram.

hot pepper sauce (recipe follows)
2 cups cold cooked brown rice or 2 cups cooked leftover Grainola
16 oz vegetable oil for frying
pinch Mock MSG I (optional)
cracker crumbs
1 Tbs cornstarch

HOT PEPPER SAUCE
1/2 cup thick tomato sauce
1 Tbs hot pepper flakes
2 Tbs cooking oil
1/4 tsp chili powder
1/8 tsp ground black pepper

FOR SAUCE
Heat oil in skillet. When oil has started moving, drop in a pepper flake to test. If oil foams around flake, remove oil from heat and pour over flakes in bowl. Oil must be hot enough to get a sizzling sound out of flakes to release hot flavor. Put everything else in bowl and start grinder.

FOR GRINDER
1. Work cornstarch into rice to give it more cohesiveness.
2. Open palm of hand and put a large tablespoon inside, shape rice like a half-ball. Put a half-teaspoon of sauce inside. With free hand, cover with more rice and form a firm ball, making sure sauce doesn't leak out.
3. Roll balls gently in cracker crumbs and shape as you would a snowball until crumbs are firmly packed.
4. Heat oil in a small deep kettle or tempura cooker until it is almost smoking (cooking at this temperature prevents balls from absorbing oil).
5. Lower 2 balls at a time into oil and cook til brown, about 2 mins.
6. Dry on toweling and arrange 3 or 4 inside split, toasted baguette bread loaves or hoagie bread buns.
7. Top with minced scallion, shredded radish or a splendid, snappy Szechuanian touch: fresh radish sprouts.

"Pork is a questionable buy. The tantalizing fresh pink color is an indication of nothing, since it is usually induced by a tranquilizer injection into the animal before slaughter, rather than by good health . . ."
— Nikki and David Goldbeck, *The Supermarket Handbook*, Harper & Row, 1973

It is perfectly legal for "All Meat" frankfurters to contain 10% added water, and 5% sodium nitrite or sodium nitrate. This chemical has been found to depress action of the thyroid gland, which makes proper utilization of vitamin A impossible.

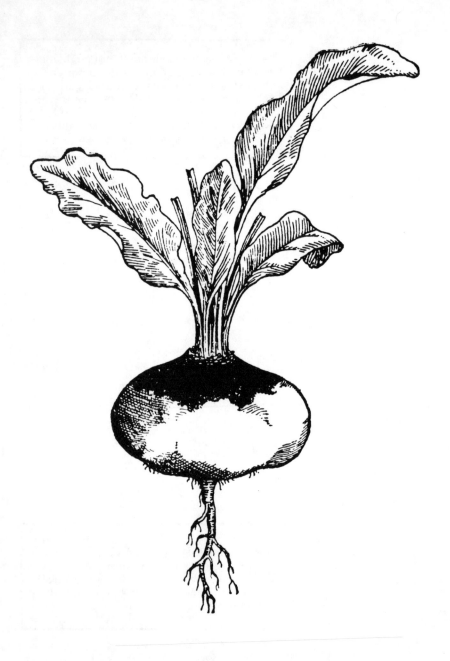

UNREAL VEAL

HALF-CALF
De-calfinated Veal Scallopine

1 cup of Tofu, mashed
1 large raw egg
1 large Tbs fresh chopped parsley
1/2 tsp garlic powder
1 tsp tamari soy sauce
1 medium onion, finely chopped
1 medium sized boiled potato, jacket removed
1 tsp celery salt
1 Tbs mushroom powder
cornmeal

1. Combine all of the ingredients well.
2. Shape into cutlets, adding further binding in the form of Bum Crumbs or any dry bread crumbs.
3. Dredge in cornmeal or Bum Crumbs and bake on a greased griddle or baking dish in a moderate (325°) oven til brown. *Note:* 99-44/100% vegetarians might like to add a meaty bottom note to this dish by brushing baking pan with melted suet instead.
4. Serve with Sprout Tomato Sauce (see THE MOCK CROCK).

3/4 cup ground cooked Gluten
unbaked pie crust
1 small finely shredded onion
1 bunch watercress
1/2 cup Mock-Veal Marinade
1 tsp Homemade Poultry Seasoning
1-1/2 cups freshly mashed potatoes

    1. Soak Gluten in marinade for 4 or more hours. Drain and squeeze dry. Mix with onion and seasonings.
    2. Prepare your favorite whole-grain pie crust recipe and roll out as square as possible. Spread with potato, then with seasoned Gluten. Sprinkle with half of the watercress (with or without stems) coarsely chopped. Roll up as you would a jelly-roll. Make decorative steam-holes with tines of a table fork and brush with melted butter or oil.
    3. Bake 10 mins in 425° oven; lower heat to 350° and bake 15 mins more.
    4. Serve with additional mashed potatoes and garnish with remaining sprigs of cress.

FAKE STEAKS
Two Sham Schnitzels

I
2 cups chick-pea flour
1 qt vegetable broth and 2 cups Mock-Veal Marinade
1 tsp each: fennel seed, salt, chopped Italian parsley

    1. Heat water, herbs and salt until lukewarm. Gradually and very slowly stir in flour, with saucepan over burner, keeping a steady stirring pace so gravy does not turn lumpy.
    2. Continue stirring until flour begins to get thick and starts to separate from kettle.

3. Immediately put into glass containers to form. Remove from jars when chilled and slice very thin.

4. Bake on a heavy griddle or saute in small amount of vegetable oil til browned.

Serve with a boat of Lumpy Gravy or Sprout Tomato sauce (see THE MOCK CROCK).

II
1-1/2 cups prepared Gluten cut into scallops
1/4 cup ground millet mixed with 4 Tbs dry milk powder
1/4 tsp each paprika and turmeric
1 egg, beaten
1/2 tsp dried rosemary
1/4 cup Mock-Veal Marinade
1/4 cup broth
1/4 cup Bum Crumbs
2 Tbs olive oil
fresh rosemary for garnish

1. Soak scallops in marinade 4 hours or longer. Drain and dip in beaten egg, then in millet mixture. Set aside 20 mins til coating hardens, then dip in egg and then in Bum Crumbs.

2. Heat 2 Tbs olive oil in large skillet, set scallops in skillet and place in a 325° oven for 20 mins.

3. Meanwhile combine marinade and broth with 2 Tbs Insta-Steer Starter and 1 Tbs whole-wheat flour in blender container. Process til smooth. Heat, stirring to prevent lumping, until smooth.

4. Serve steaks under steak sauce — with a garnish of fresh sprays of rosemary, if such a flourish is possible.

about 1/2 lb prepared Gluten
1 beaten egg

BREADING MIXTURE
wheat germ
paprika
grated parmesan cheese
Vegebutcher Salt
1/2 tsp Italian herb seasoning
dry milk powder (about 1/3 cup in all)

SAUCE
1 Tbs potato starch
1 tsp good quality Italian seasoning
1 tsp garlic juice
1/2 chopped onion
chopped parsley
1-1/2 cups organic seasoning broth
1/2 shredded green pepper
freshly grated parmesan or romano cheese

1. Slice prepared Gluten into cutlets about 1/4" thick.
2. Dip in beaten egg and then in breading mixture. Dredge liberally.
3. Arrange slices in a well-greased baking pan or skillet and brown in oven at 350° for 20 mins.
4. Process all sauce ingredients in blender and pour into saucepan. Heat over moderate flame until thickened, stirring constantly.
5. Pour sauce over browned cutlets and return to oven. Bake an additional 15 mins. Sprinkle with grated cheese and serve.

MOCKING BIRDS I
Unreal Veal Birds in a Real Veal Sauce

9 scallops of prepared Gluten
9 thin slices of Swiss or gruyere cheese
freshly ground black pepper
2 Tbs olive oil
1 bay leaf
6 small onions, peeled
1/2 cup dry white wine or vermouth
2 large tomatoes
1/2 tsp Vegebutcher salt
1 Tbs flour mixed with 1 Tbs Insta-Steer Savory or miso and 1 Tbs broth

1. Place one slice of cheese on each Gluten slice, sprinkle lightly with pepper. Roll up with Gluten on outside; tie with clean string or secure with toothpicks.

2. Heat oil and bay leaf in a large skillet, add "veal" rolls in a single layer; saute, turning until golden-brown all over.

3. Add onions, salt, pepper, and 1/2 cup wine. Simmer, covered, for 30 mins or until tender.

4. Pour boiling water over tomatoes; let stand several mins until skin peels off easily with knife. Quarter, remove seeds and add during last 10 mins of cooking.

5. Remove birds with slotted spoon to serving platter. Remove string or wooden picks.

6. Spoon vegetables around birds. In skillet, add flour mixture to pan juices. Bring to a boil, stirring, and boil 3 mins. Pour over birds and serve to six.

"Americans annually drink up the amount of grain that could feed 25 million people a year"
— *New York Times*, Dec. 11, 1974

MOCKING BIRDS II
Unreal Veal Birds Under a Glaze

3/4 lb eggplant, approximately
1/4 cup olive or vegetable oil
1 cup Mock-Veal Marinade
1 cup cooked Vegemeat
1/4 cup minced onion plus 1 crushed chopped clove garlic
2 Tbs finely chopped parsley
1/4 cup almond meal

1. Peel eggplant and slice lengthwise into 1/8"-thick slices. Soak slices 1 hour or more in marinade.

2. Squeeze (gently) slices dry and blot out any remaining moisture with paper toweling. Reserve marinade.

3. Heat half of the oil in a large skillet and saute onion and garlic til soft, add Vegemeat, heat briefly and remove from burner.

4. Lay slices of eggplant on cutting board and spoon equal portions of filling in center of each. Roll up birds to enclose filling and arrange in a single layer on bottom of a greased ovenproof dish or casserole.

5. Put reserved marinade into smallest saucepan you have and boil down til syrupy so just enough remains to coat the birds (if not enough remains, replenish marinade or add milk). Pour over birds, sprinkle with almond meal, parsley and remaining olive oil. Bake briefly (8-10 mins) in a very hot oven (475°) until nut crumbs are browned.

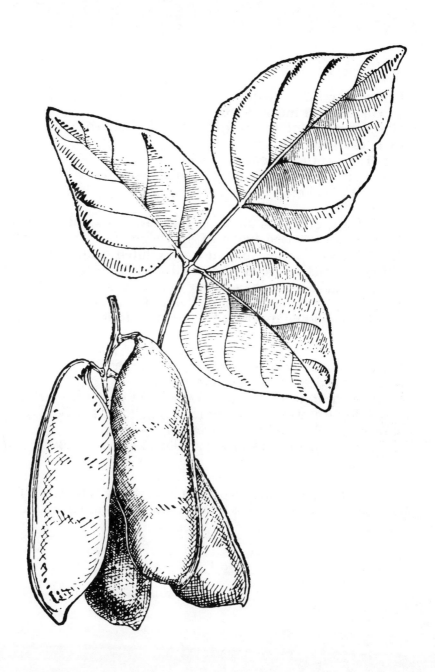

FRUIT STEW
For Frugivores

1-1/2 cups minced onion
1/4 cup dairy or mock butter
3 lbs prepared Gluten cut into 1-1/2'' cubes (pre-soaked in Mock-Veal Marinade)
1 cup dry wine
4 lbs fresh quinces (see *Note* below)
1 tsp honey, 1/2 tsp salt, pinch cinnamon
peel of 1/2 orange

1. Saute onions in butter in a generous-sized skillet until they are golden. Transfer with slotted spoon to a flameproof casserole with tight-fitting lid.
2. In same skillet, brown 3 lbs Gluten (adding more butter or oil while sauteing) which has been squeezed dry of marinade juices. Transfer to casserole.
3. Deglaze skillet by pouring marinade and wine into pan and scraping up any brown bits. Transfer all of this to the casserole.
4. Bring liquid to a boil, cover casserole and cook in a preheated 325° oven for 30 mins.
5. Meanwhile, peel, quarter and core 4 lbs quinces and halve each quarter lengthwise. Add quinces to baking dish with 1 tsp honey and spices. Put peel of orange in center of the mixture.
6. Bake stew for 1 hour, covered. Let cool and chill for 2 days.
7. Return casserole to burner. Bring liquid to a boil, transfer to a preheated slow oven (325°) and bake covered for 45 mins.
8. Serve with black olives and break open a package of banana chips as an added fillip.

Note: Tart apples (Baldwins) are an acceptable surrogate for quince but if apples are used, reduce sweetness (omit honey) and shorten cooking time by 15 mins.

APPLE SAUSAGE
Mock Veal Franks for the Vegebrunch

1-1/2 cups cooked soybeans
1/2 cup dried apple slices
1/2 cup nut meal (peanut, cashew, walnut or a mixture)
1/2 tsp Vegebutcher salt
1 egg
1/2 tsp poultry seasoning
wheat germ if needed
oil for sauteing, 1 Tbs or more as needed

1. Put the beans through meat grinder alternating with dried apple.
2. Combine mixture with 1/4 cup nut meal and seasoning and blend in egg. Shape into small sausages, adding more nut meal or wheat germ as needed for body.
3. Brown sausages over medium heat in large skillet, turning to cook all sides. Good with or without the sauce below and some raisin toast, too.

SAUCE
1. Soak 1/2 cup chopped dried apples in 1 cup apple cider overnight.
2. Drain slices. Put cider in a greased saucepan and bring to a boil. Boil until thick and syrupy and reduced by more than half. Add 1/4 cup maple syrup and chopped apples and pour over sausages.

"There is no regular USDA monitoring of salmonella or other contaminants in U.S. meat and poultry plants . . . the only person who checks bacteria counts in most meat plants is a local health official who comes once a year."

— Harrison Wellford
Sowing the Wind, Bantam, 1971

SHAM LAMB

BUM BROCHETTE I

2 cups prepared cubed Gluten
1 cup Mock-Lamb Marinade
1 cup cooked (but not too soft) chestnuts
2 Tbs freshly ground sesame seeds
1/2 cup Bumstock II or well flavored vegetable broth
Vegebutcher salt and pepper to taste

    1. Marinate cubed Gluten for at least 4 hours or overnight so that "meaty" flavor will penetrate cubes.
    2. Thread Gluten on skewers, alternating with whole chestnuts, and arrange threaded skewers on sheet of aluminum foil spread on a cookie sheet.
    3. Brush liberally with marinade and bake in 375° oven brushing and turning often for 20 mins.
    4. Combine any remaining marinade with Bumstock, seasoning and seeds and bring to a boil in small saucepan. Boil til thick and syrupy. Pass this around with the brochettes as a dipping sauce. Serve over 100% Vegetarian Noodles (see ON THE SIDE) and sesame crackers.

1/2 cup or more of each:
    cubed cucumber
    whole water chestnuts
    2″ chunks of fresh celery, celeriac or fennel
    chunks of watermelon rind (white part only)
    wedges of grapefruit
    chunks of raw zucchini
soybean mustard, 1 cup or more (see THE MOCK CROCK)
1/4 cup or more ground brazil nuts and grated grapefruit peel

    1. Thread the above vegetables and fruit on metal skewers and brush with the mustard.
    2. Roll kebabs in nut meal and peel. Broil, watching carefully. Turn and broil on opposite side.
    3. Serve with more soybean mustard at room temperature. Great with curried couscous. Good with any Grainola.

> Meat, fish and fowl, according to the *Pesiticides Monitoring Journal*, contain more than twice as many parts per million residue of pesticides than does the second highest category (dairy products).

2 cups of unpoached Gluten
1/2 cup red and green peppers in strips
1/2 cup zucchini or watermelon rind (only inner white part) cut in match-
    stick size.
1 leek or 2-3 green onions chopped
1 large garlic clove, mashed and minced
chopped parsley and grated orange peel
1/4 cup chopped peanuts
1/4 cup whole peanuts
1/4 cup peanut butter
1 cup Mock Milk and 1 cup Bumstock II or vegetable broth
1 tsp soy sauce
2 Tbs flour
3 Tbs vegetable oil (peanut preferred)
1 tsp curry powder
1/2 tsp cumin powder and 1/4 tsp turmeric

1. When Gluten is squeezed of its starch and you are ready to poach, slice into strips as thinly as possible with as sharp a knife as you can muster. Poach as usual according to master recipe, replacing poaching water in part or completely with Mock-Lamb Marinade.

2. Meanwhile, heat oil in a wok or large skillet, add the vegetables (reserving peel and parsley) and stir-fry until soft. Gradually stir in flour and then gradually add peanut meal. Pour in a bit of the broth and, stirring all the while, alternate broth with milk and stir til thickened and smooth. Put into blender with peanut butter and process til smooth.

3. Return sauce to skillet or put in saucepan. Add cumin and curry powders, soy sauce and "lamb" strips. When heated thoroughly, serve with rice and top with whole peanuts, grated orange peel and parsley. Good (with or without the lamb) as a second-day chunky soup.

ROAST LEG OF LIMA
With Gravy

1-1/2 cups cooked lima beans
1 finely shredded onion
3/4 cup tomato juice
3/4 tsp crushed rosemary
1 tsp Vegebutcher salt
1/2 tsp garlic flakes
2 Tbs dairy or mock butter or olive oil
1 beaten egg
1 Tbs water
1-1/2 cups whole wheat bread crumbs or Bum Crumbs
crushed cracker crumbs

1. Mash beans and press through a sieve or put into a ricer.
2. Add remaining ingredients, except egg and crumbs, and mix thoroughly.
3. Add bread crumbs using just enough to make a mixture firm enough to mold.
4. Shape, with wet hands, into a large leg and dredge with remaining bread crumbs.
5. Roll "leg" in egg-water mixture, then in crushed cracker crumbs. Place in a medium-sized roaster or buttered casserole.
6. Bake uncovered at 425° for about 35 mins until nicely browned. Turn twice during cooking, lowering heat to 375° and covering with foil if browning proceeds too quickly.

Note: You may make smaller "legs" instead, and bake them at the same temperature for only 15 mins, turning once. Insert wooden sticks near the end of cooking time (to facilitate post-baking eating) thereby creating the world's only lima bean with drumsticks.

GRAVY (Lemon flavored)
2 Tbs butter
2 Tbs flour or potato starch
2 egg yolks
3/4 cup light cream or yogurt cream cheese

2 Tbs lemon juice
chopped chives (garnish, optional)
1 cup Bumstock or vegetable bouillon

1. Melt butter, blend in flour, stir constantly, cooking about 3 mins.
2. Gradually blend in stock until thickened.
3. Beat together yolks and cream or cheese. Add to hot sauce, stirring briskly. Cook gently, briefly.
4. Add lemon juice and chives. Pass in separate gravy boat.

"Sellers . . . may adulterate the meat with cochineal (a red dye from ground insects), coal-tar dyes, or sodium nitrite. Sodium nitrite, frequently found in hamburger meat, changes in the stomach to nitrous acid, which can cause biological mutations."
— Gary Null and staff, *Body Pollution*, Arco Publishing Co., 1973

1-1/2 cups bulgur
2 cups Bumstock II or vegetable broth
1 cup chopped onion
1 tsp Vegebutcher salt
1/2 tsp pepper
1-1/3 cups coarsely chopped walnuts
1/4 cup butter and 1/4 cup olive oil
1-1/2 cups chopped leek or onion
2 cups chopped mushroom
1/2 tsp each salt and cinnamon
pinch ground allspice
1/4 cup finely chopped walnuts
2 Tbs sesame seed
3 Tbs oil or butter
8 oz plain or mint-flavored yogurt

1. Soak bulgur in broth for 25 mins.
2. Drain, squeeze dry and mix with 1-1/2 cups chopped onion, salt and pepper. Put through food grinder twice.
3. In skillet, melt butter and oil (1/4 cup each) and saute 1-1/3 cups walnuts until browned. Transfer to dish with slotted spoon.
4. Add 1 cup minced onion to skillet and saute 5 mins. Add mushrooms, salt, cinnamon, allspice and saute 2 mins.
5. Add walnuts, salt and pepper to taste and combine thoroughly.
6. Butter a square 1-1/2 qt baking dish (or a clay cooker of equal size) and press the mixture in firmly.
7. Slice through the mixture to make 8 squares. Press remaining walnuts and sesame seeds into the top of the kibbeh and sprinkle with remaining 2 Tbs of oil or butter.
8. Bake in a preheated 350° oven for 35 mins. Raise heat to 450° and bake 5 mins longer.
9. Serve warm with a cool dish of mint-flavored yogurt. Or, if you opted for yogurt plain, add a ring of pickled cherries (a traditional real-meat garnish in Germany and Belgium).

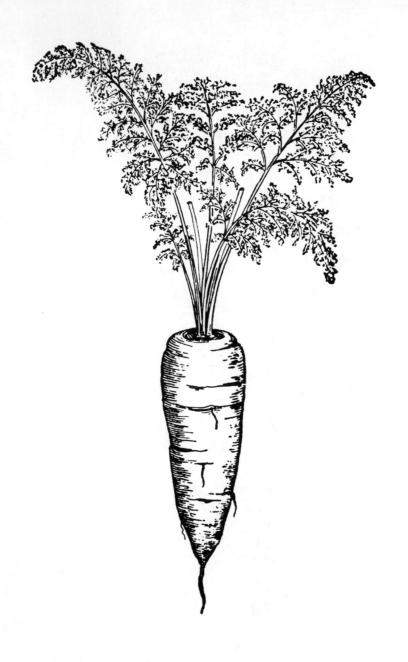

CON GAME

BUM BUNNY
Hasenpfeffer for Humanitarian Harriers

8 serving pieces of prepared Gluten
3/4 cup dry red wine
1/4 cup cider vinegar
1/2 minced onion
1 Tbs mixed whole pickling spices
1 tsp salt
1/2 tsp freshly ground pepper
Bum Crumbs for dredging
1 diced slice of suet (or substitute 2 Tbs olive oil)
1 Tbs butter or soy butter
1/2 onion (the mate to the one above), sliced thin
1 clove of mashed garlic
1 Tbs brown sugar
1/2 cup Bumstock II or any broth
1/2 Tbs lemon juice
1/4 cup yogurt, liquefied cottage cheese or sour cream

1. Mix wine, vinegar, onion, spices in a large mixing bowl and marinate Gluten pieces for 24 hours, turning now and then.
2. Remove Gluten, pat dry and dredge with Bum Crumbs.
3. Heat suet and butter in a heavy pot (Dutch oven, electric crock pot, ovenproof casserole, etc) and brown the breaded "Bum Bunny" over a moderate heat. Remove, and brown onion and garlic in same pot, stir in sugar and cook 3 mins.
4. To pan juices, add Bumstock and reserved marinade.
5. Return Gluten to pan and bring liquids to a boil; reduce heat, cover tightly and simmer about 1 hour, or bake in a 325° oven. When done, stir in yogurt, cheese or cream and lemon juice. Serve on a bed of shredded lettuce and carrot with Bunny Bummers (recipe follows) atop.

BUNNY BUMMERS

Make up your favorite (keep it simple) pie crust or cracker dough recipe, roll out as though for crackers and cut out with Easter bunny cookie cutter. Bake til browned in a moderate oven.

Note: If you'd like the cracker to echo the Hasenpfeffer seasoning, grind some pickling spice to a fine powder and add 1/2 - 3/4 tsp to your dough before rolling out.

POTTED MEAT WITH PECAN MILK
Mock Duck Baked in a Flower Pot

1/4 tsp each, sweet game herbs: basil, marjoram, sage, mint, savory
1 tsp Vegebutcher salt
2 cups fresh cooked peas
1 whole leek, chopped
1/4 cup finely minced pecan nutmeats
1/4 cup sunflower meal or fine whole-wheat crumbs
2 slightly beaten eggs
4 Tbs olive oil
3/4 cup pecan milk (below)
1 tsp blackstrap molasses or honey
1 large clean flower pot (terra cotta)

    1. Scrub pot and wash in dishwasher. Dry.
    2. Puree or mash peas and combine with pecan milk (puree 1/3 cup raw pecans with 1 cup soy or dairy milk or water), add remaining ingredients, reserve crumbs.
    3. Butter flower pot and pack "meat" inside. You may sprinkle buttered insides with crumbs or use them after packing meat.
    4. Chill 1 hour. Bake in a preheated 350° oven 40 mins.
    5. Cool slightly, turn out, slice and serve in a napkin-lined Bread Basket.

LAME DUCK
Soft Duck Patties in a Dieters' Nut Sauce

PATTIES
1 cup rolled oats, finely ground
3 duck eggs (chicken eggs may be used)
1/2 cup finely ground almonds
1/2 tsp ground celery seed
1 tsp chives chopped
1 tsp poultry seasoning
2 Tbs garlic-flavored oil

1. Mix all ingredients and form into patties.
2. Fry in oil until golden brown on both sides. Set aside while making sauce.

NUT SAUCE
1 cup skim milk plus 1 cup yogurt
1 Tbs vegetable oil
1/2 cup soy powder plus 1/2 cup powdered milk
2/3 cup chopped almonds
2 Tbs chopped onion
1 Tbs Vegebutcher salt
1 Tbs chopped chives
1/2 tsp paprika, plus 1/4 tsp mace

1. Put skim milk, yogurt and oil in blender and add soy powder, powdered milk, almonds and onion, salt, chives, mace and paprika.
2. Blend for 1 min, pour into saucepan and simmer 10 mins, stirring constantly. (Each Tbs has 44 calories and 3 gms complete protein).

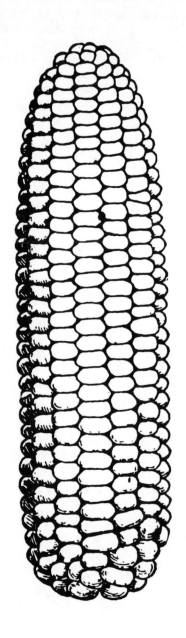

PHONEY POULTRY

MOCK DRUMSTICKS

1-1/2 lbs Vegemeat
1 egg
1/4 cup soy grits or bread crumbs
2 Tbs diced onions
2 Tbs milk
3/4 tsp garlic salt
1/8 tsp black pepper
1/4 cup wheat germ plus 1 Tbs Homemade Poultry Seasoning
2 or 3 Tbs vegetable oil

1. Combine everything except last two ingredients.
2. Mix everything thoroughly and shape into 8 individual rolls, or croquettes.
3. Put wheat germ and seasoning in a paper bag. Moisten each drumstick with water and gently shake in seasoned coating til well covered.
4. Heat oil in a large skillet and when mustard seed in the seasoning pops, add drumsticks. Cook over medium heat or put in oven to brown. Brown on all sides in skillet or bake in oven for 20 mins at 350°. Remove and insert wooden skewer with paper ruffle. Serve with a Mock Mustard (see The Mock Crock) or Banana Stuffing for Mock Chicken (see ON THE SIDE).

101

GOBBLER COBBLER

1 cup thinly sliced "turkey" (raw rounds of turnip)
1/2 cup sliced leek or sliced yellow onion
2 large stalks celery, shredded
3 large eggs
1/4 stick dairy or soy butter
2 cups scalded dairy or soy milk
1 tsp poultry seasoning
1/2 tsp Vegebutcher salt
freshly grated parmesan cheese, poultry-seasoned bread crumbs, paprika

1. Lightly saute onion, celery and turnip in butter over moderate heat until tender.

2. In a bowl, beat eggs til foamy and stir in milk, cooked vegetables, poultry seasoning and salt.

3. Transfer mixture to a greased 1 qt baking dish. Sprinkle top with cheese and seasoned bread crumbs, set dish in a deep baking pan, add boiling water to cover 2/3 of sides of dish and bake in 350° oven for 45 mins or until well set in the center. Serve with cranberry beans or Mock Giblet Gravy (see THE MOCK CROCK) and toast.

NULLO POLLO
Mock Chicken Dumplings in Curry Sauce

CURRY SAUCE
1 apple, 1 onion, 2 stalks celery
1-1/2 cups Mock-Chicken Marinade
2 Tbs soy flour
1 tsp curry powder
1/2 tsp Mock MSG I
2 Tbs sesame or apricot oil
1 tsp sea salt
3 cups sprouted chick-peas

1. Mince or shred apple, onion and celery. Saute in vegetable oil.

2. Add marinade to sauteed vegetables.

3. Mix flour, curry powder, salt and Mock MSG into paste. Stir paste into vegetables. Stir in sprouts. Simmer 20 mins and serve with Dumplings (see below).

MOCK CHICKEN DUMPLINGS
10 small onions
3 Tbs soy butter with pinch of sugar
1/2 cup Mock-Chicken Marinade
1 cup chick-pea flour, 1 cup whole-grain flour
2 tsp baking powder plus 1 tsp sea salt
3 Tbs soy butter plus 3 Tbs vegetable oil
2/3 cup mock or dairy milk
grated cumin-flavored cheese (or sharp cheddar)
caraway seeds

1. Saute onions in 3 Tbs butter with sugar. Add marinade and simmer, covered, for 20 mins. Transfer onions to paper towels and let cool.

2. Sift together, flours, salt, baking powder, in small bowl. Blend in butter and oil til mixture is mealy.

3. Stir in milk gradually until mixture becomes dough-like. Transfer to floured board and knead until no longer sticky. Roll 1/4'' thick and cut into ten small squares.

4. Spread each square with dab of soft butter, put onion in center and sprinkle with grated cheese. Bring corners of dough up over onion and press together.

5. Brush dumplings with 1 egg beaten with 1 Tbs milk and sprinkle with seeds. Transfer to buttered baking sheet and bake in preheated hot oven (425°) 20 mins or until golden.

FAKE FISH

BANANA FISH

3 or 4 large near-ripe bananas
1 lemon, juiced, with peel grated and dried
1 tsp butter
1 tsp seafood seasoning powder or shrimp boil powder or fines herbes powder
1 Tbs flour
6 large fresh whole mushrooms
1/4 to 1/2 cup whole-wheat bread crumbs
1 Tbs olive (or other vegetable) oil
salt and pepper to taste
1/2 cup Bumstock I and 1/2 cup milk

    1. Butter a medium-sized ramekin or oval porcelain roaster or fish-shaped baking dish.
    2. "Filet" bananas and set aside short irregular end pieces.
    3. Spread each large center slice with butter and press slices of mushroom into spread to cover surface.
    4. Put slices together as though making a sandwich.
    5. Arrange the 3 or 4 steaks side by side in buttered dish and sprinkle with teaspoon of lemon juice.
    6. Melt butter and olive oil and stir in flour, stirring until smooth and blended. Add seasonings and 1 tsp grated lemon peel, then broth and milk (if you are not in a hurry, heat first for a smoother sauce). Stir til smooth and creamy.
    7. Cover fish filets with sauce, sprinkle on crumbs and bake at 325° for 20 mins. Serve with Noodle Fry or Herbed Coconut (see ON THE SIDE) and garnish with radish leaves.

1 cup chick-pea flour
2 tsp seafood seasoning
2 tsp turmeric
3/4 tsp cayenne
1 Tbs sugar
3 tsp peanut oil
nori, 3 sheets
3 to 4 firm bananas with clean, unsprayed, naturally ripened skins
4 Tbs peanut oil
1/2 tsp cumin seed
1/2 tsp mustard seed

1. In a small bowl, mix chick-pea flour, sugar and 1/2 tsp cayenne with 1 tsp each turmeric and salt. Add the 3 tsp oil. Blend well with fingers until crumbly.

2. Slice stem ends from bananas; do not peel. Cut into thirds, crosswise. Make a slit about halfway down the middle of each chunk. Stuff with as much chick-pea mixture as possible.

3. Heat the 4 Tbs oil and to it add the cumin, mustard seed and remaining cayenne, salt and turmeric. When mustard seed pops, add banana chunks one at a time on their sides until bottom of pan is covered.

4. Turn heat quite low, cover pan, shake twice to spread oil over all. Turn banana bits after six minutes (using fork). Cook 6 more mins.

5. Eat skin and all. Serve with saffron-flavored couscous or some banana-yellow millet plus toasted sheets of nori.

According to a National Shellfish Sanitation Program report, almost half (40%) of the seafood processing plants inspected had unsanitary conditions, 27% of which were considered very significant. (1974)

FAKE FRIED CLAMS
With a Cold Clam Sauce

CLAMS
1 cup of whole or halved unsalted cashews

BATTER:
1 beaten egg
1/2 cup water or fish stock (Bumstock I)
enough flour to make a moderately sticky batter (a half-vegetable flour batter
    is fine)
oil for deep frying

1. Prepare batter and heat oil for frying in tempura cooker, kettle, electric fry pan, or wok to 300°.
2. Toast "clam meat" 15 mins in a low oven (below 300°).
3. Dip nuts in batter and pick out with a small spoon. Be sure batter completely covers nutmeat but remove any excess from spoon before transferring to cooking pan. Turn nuts once for even browning.
4. Drain on paper toweling and keep warm in covered dish while you prepare sauce.

COLD CLAM SAUCE
1. Put 1 room-temperature egg into blender container with 1 tsp fines herbes or seafood seasoning, 1 tsp salt or Vegebutcher salt, pinch dry mustard, 2 Tbs fresh lemon juice, 1/4 cup olive oil. Blend on "chop" for 10 seconds.
2. Remove lid of blender and, in a steady stream, add 3/4 cup additional olive oil (you may replace part with another vegetable oil such as soybean or safflower) while on "chop."
3. Turn off blender, and add 1/4 cup finely minced fresh parsley, then blend for 10 seconds and spoon into small serving bowl.

SNAIL DOUGH:
1 Tbs dry yeast
1/2 tsp honey or sugar
1 cup lukewarm Bumstock I
2 cups fish flour (unbleached white flour and 1/2 cup vegetable flour — soy, chick-pea, lima — plus 4 Tbs kelp powder)
pinches of salt, nutmeg, parsley flakes
1/4 cup milk powder
1 slightly beaten egg
4 Tbs butter or vegetable oil

    1. Sprinkle yeast over 1/4 cup lukewarm water, add sugar and set aside until bubbly.
    2. Combine milk powder, flours and seasonings in mixing bowl.
    3. Add yeast-water combination to dry ingredients and alternately add oil and beaten egg. Gradually add remaining broth.
    4. Beat and knead mixture in the bowl. It should be stiff enough to handle. If too moist, add extra flour or wheat germ.
    5. Cover bowl. Let rise in a warm spot until doubled in bulk, about 45 mins.
    6. Turn dough out onto floured board. Knead a few times for 5-10 mins. Roll out to 1/2" thickness.
    7. Cut into two equal-sized rectangles and sprinkle each with a "snail" filling as follows:

1/4 cup of lightly steamed and chopped spinach
1/4 cup cooked chopped hizichi (seaweed) or Seedmeat
1/4 cup freshly grated parmesan cheese
1 tsp each, Vegebutcher salt, seafood seasoning or fines herbes seasoning
3 Tbs each olive oil and mock or dairy butter, melted

    8. Roll up each rectangle (as for a jelly-roll). Chill slightly (about 1 hour) to facilitate handling. Slice into 1/2"-thick slices and place side by side on greased baking sheet.
    9. Bake snails for 15 mins at 400°. Serve with Greenbutcher Gravy I or II (see THE MOCK CROCK).

HANGTOWN HOAX

3 cups cooked mock oyster (salsify or oyster plant)
3 eggs
1/4 cup olive oil
1 tsp Vegebutcher salt
1/2 cup raw cream or thick cashew milk
1 tsp seafood seasoning
1/4 cup Bum Crumbs
1/2 tsp Mock MSG I

1. Put the salsify through a sieve to induce a mushy consistency.
2. Beat eggs well and combine with mock oyster stuff, cream, oil, salt, seafood seasoning and Mock MSG.
3. Pour into a greased ovenproof fish mold or shell mold (if the latter, sprinkle with buttered Bum Crumbs) and bake at 325° about 35 mins. Serve with Fake Pfannkuchen (see ON THE SIDE).

Note: Salsify, whose extraordinary taproots produce the oyster-flavored mock meat above, is one of the most nutritious of all the root crops. If you grow your own, try some simply steamed and buttered.

"The carbohydrate and mineral content of canned tuna is low . . . persons on a low-sodium diet should probably *steer clear of canned tuna* altogether. The average sodium content of a 3-1/2 oz. serving was 478 mg. - near the *maximum daily allowance . . .*"
— *Consumer Reports*, Nov., 1974

2 Tbs gelatin
1/4 cup cold Bumstock I
3-1/4 cups hot Bumstock I
2 Tbs capers
2 or 3 Tbs lemon juice
1/2 tsp each, summer savory and dry mustard
1 cup cooked hizichi (or a chopped, cooked seaweed such as wakame, nori, dulse)

1. Soak gelatin in cold stock and dissolve it in the hot stock.
2. Add capers, herbs and correct seasoning.
3. Wet a fish-shaped mold in cold water and meanwhile chill aspic until it begins to thicken.
4. Spoon one layer of aspic into mold, cover with drained strips of hizichi, and top with final layer of aspic. Chill.
5. Unmold aspic and serve very cold with fresh "eels" (long strips of cucumber peel) and shredded red or white radish. Plus mayonnaise, of course (for a Mock Mayonnaise, see THE MOCK CROCK).

EGGPLANT FISH
With Eggplant Caviar

FISH
1 eggplant
flour
3 Tbs olive oil
salt and pepper
lemon wedges

1. Peel one eggplant, halve lengthwise and remove and discard seeds.
2. Cut each half lengthwise into 1/4" slices and cut slices into 3-inch lengths, tapering them into fish shapes.
3. Spread slices on paper towels, sprinkle with salt, and flatten under a light weight for 30 mins.

4. Pat slices dry with paper toweling and dust with flour.

5. In a large skillet, saute slices on both sides in olive oil in several batches, adding more oil if necessary until they are golden.

6. Drain slices on towels, sprinkle with salt and pepper and serve hot with lemon wedges and the caviar below.

CAVIAR
1 large eggplant
2 Tbs minced scallion and 2 Tbs catsup
1/4 cup olive oil
1 Tbs red wine vinegar
1 tsp Vegebutcher salt and 1/4 tsp freshly ground pepper
1/2 tsp Mock MSG II (optional)

1. With a fork, pierce skin of eggplant and place in rimmed pan. Bake in 400° oven for 1 hour until soft.

2. Cool; split skin and scoop out insides.

3. Add all other ingredients and stir until creamy. Serve at room temperature with "fish," plus bowls of any hot Grainola.

> Thanks to the "purse-seine" fishing method favored by the U.S. tuna industry, an estimated 200,000 dolphins are slaughtered every year. They become entangled in the giant nets, and those which might escape often refuse to leave their fellows in distress . . . those who eat tuna and feed it to their cats give the fishing industry their powerful influence in the Department of Commerce, which should be protecting the dolphin under the Marine Mammal Act of 1972.
> — *Let's Live* Magazine, Dec., 1974

very finely chopped or scissored lettuce
very finely grated carrot
chopped or minced green onion
tahini (sesame butter)
tomato
peanut butter
tomato juice, fresh lemon juice or yogurt
pinch cayenne and paprika
soft, fresh sliced bread

1. Mix enough yogurt, tomato juice or lemon juice to thin peanut butter and flavor it.
2. Toss together onion, carrot and lettuce. Combine with first mixture.
3. With butterfly cookie or canape cutter (or cut a simple tracing pattern from light cardboard) cut out butterfly shapes from soft fresh bread. Spread with sesame tahini (a good butter substitute) and then with the mock shrimp spread (the carrots give the appearance and taste of shrimp when combined with the nut butters and lettuce).
4. Sprinkle with cayenne and paprika and toast lightly in a toaster oven. Serve with wedges of tomato and tomato-juice cocktails for a light lunch, or a late breakfast.

PLAIN SHRIMP TOAST
Skip butterfly-making step, spread the Mock-Shrimp mix on plain toast or toasted English muffins.

BUTTERFLY SHRIMP II
Or Plain Shrimp Toast II

4 slices sandwich bread
1/2 lb potato, boiled with skin, peeled and mashed
1 small carrot, peeled, cooked *al dente* and chopped fine
1/2 leek, chopped (or 2 chopped scallions)
1 tsp Vegebutcher salt or seafood seasoning
1/8 tsp fresh ground pepper
1 egg beaten with 1/2 tsp salt
Bum Crumbs
oil and cornstarch

1. Mix everything except bread with 1 Tbs oil and 1 tsp cornstarch.
2. Cut large butterfly silhouettes out of bread slices and brush with beaten egg.
3. Spread shrimp mixture over face of bread cut-outs and press bread into breading or fine crumbs.
4. Fry face down in hot oil for 10 seconds, then turn to other side until bread is golden brown.

PLAIN SHRIMP TOAST
Spread on uncut slightly stale bread slices and cook as above.

SEMI-PLAIN SHRIMP TOAST
Spread over pre-cooked or thawed frozen waffles and cook as above.

Serve with Small Fry I (see ON THE SIDE) with a garnish of fresh broccoli leaves or finely scissored lettuce.

PIZZA
1 tsp dry yeast
1/2 cup lukewarm tomato juice
1 tsp honey (optional)
1 tsp Vegebutcher salt and 2 tsp paprika
1-1/2 tsp fresh or dried rosemary
4 Tbs unrefined oil, preferably olive oil (for taste)
1-1/2 cups fish flour (whole-wheat flour mixed with 4 Tbs kelp or other pow-
    dered seaweed)

1. Dissolve yeast in tomato juice and let stand until foamy.
2. Add honey, salt, half of rosemary and 1 Tbs oil. Stir in yeast and fish flour.
Knead dough briefly on floured board.
3. Put 1 Tbs oil in 10″ skillet or cake pan. Flatten dough and press into pan
as for a pizza. Every few inches make a depression with your thumb. Brush top
with remaining oil and sprinkle with remaining rosemary and paprika (for best
flavor, buy a good grade of paprika). If you wish, add the mock mollusks
described below.
4. Bake in 400° oven for 20-25 mins until browned and crisp. Serve with
soup.

MOCK MOLLUSKS
Halve, horizontally or vertically, 1 cup of drained, canned, whole water chestnuts and combine with 1 cup of spicy tomato sauce. Pour into pizza shell above
and bake per directions, with or without grated cheese and hot pepper flakes.

FAKE FISH STICKS

1 cup white or yellow corn meal
1 cup pickle brine or seaweed-soaking water
1 tsp fines herbes seasoning
2 Tbs freshly chopped parsley
2 eggs beaten with 2 Tbs water
olive oil and/or butter
1 tsp powdered seaweed
3 cups plain water
1 Tbs seafood seasoning or shrimp boil seasoning
1 chopped garlic clove
flour and fine crumbs for breading

1. Combine corn meal with sea salt and seaweed water (should be cold) in small bowl until you have a paste. Add seafood and fines herbes seasonings.

2. Bring 3 cups of water to a boil and gradually stir in the cornmeal paste; cook, stirring constantly, until thick. Then cover saucepan and cook over low heat for 10 mins.

3. Spoon mixture into a 1 quart loaf pan and pack down firmly. Cool, then chill thoroughly.

4. Remove loaf from pan and cut into sticks of any desired size. Coat sticks in flour, dip in egg-water mixture, then roll in bread crumbs.

6. Saute parsley and garlic lightly in oil. Add fish sticks and saute about 2 mins on each side or until golden and done. Serve to 6-8 people with Finless Fish Sauce or Italian Green Sauce (see THE MOCK CROCK).

> The average American ate 10 more pounds of meat in 1974 than in 1973. (The '73 average was 226 lbs.)
> — *The Business Farmer*, Winter, 1974

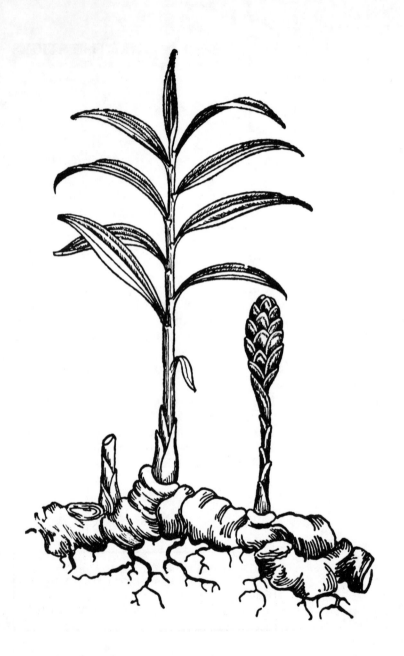

UN-INNARDS

STUFFED HEARTS FOR HERBIVORES
Cold, Carcass-less Lunch for 4

4 medium sized artichokes
1 lemon, halved
1 cup vegetable oil
4 Tbs lemon juice
1 Tbs wine vinegar
1 Tbs finely chopped shallot or scallion
2 tsp chopped sour pickles
1/4 cup chopped parsley
1 garlic clove crushed
1 Tbs sunflower seeds finely chopped
salt, freshly ground black pepper
1 cup cooked Grainola
boiling salted water

    1. Trim artichokes, clip tips of leaves and rub all surfaces with cut lemon. Slice off top third of each artichoke. Open center leaves up, turn artichokes over and press down to make leaves open fully.
    2. With spoon, scrape out choke and discard (plus inner yellow leaves). Sprinkle inside of chokes with lemon juice too. Arrange chokes in kettle so they are tightly wedged together.
    3. Add boiling water to cover, squeeze remaining half lemon over all, cover and cook 30 mins or til tender.
    4. Drain chokes upside down, turn over and fill them with Grainola. Chill.
    5. Combine remaining ingredients in a jar. Shake well and chill. Arrange stuffed hearts on individual plates, remove garlic and spoon dressing over each one. Outfit with Phoney Pfannekuchen (see ON THE SIDE) for a complete hot-and-cold running lunch for four.

BUTTERED BRAINS
Humane, Herbivorous Innards

about 1 pound of mock brains: (1 large head cauliflower, diced)
2 eggs
1 tsp Vegebutcher salt or mock MSG I
1 Tbs food yeast
1/8 tsp ground mace
1/2 cup sunflower seeds, ground
3 Tbs olive oil and 1 Tbs soy lecithin granules
3 Tbs chopped chives and finely grated lemon peel
juice of 1/4 lemon, about
2 cups cooked Seedmeat or any Grainola

   1. Blend eggs, salt, yeast, mace and dip diced "brains" in this mixture. Coat with sunflower seed meal.
   2. Heat oil in skillet and lightly saute buttered brains until golden-brown on all sides. Remove to a heated platter.
   3. Chop cauliflower core and tenderest leaves and gently steam these. Make a bed of these bottom greens, top with heated Grainola or Seedmeat, warmed brains; sprinkle with chopped chives, grated peel, lemon juice and lecithin granules. *Note:* Although it is an omissible ingredient, phosphorus-rich lecithin granules are brain food, too. (See BUM STEERS REMEDY BAR for more about lecithin.) And cauliflower is a low-calorie appetite-stimulant rich in calcium and sulphur. There is twice as much ascorbic acid in the outer leaves and core of the cauliflower as there is in the inner curd, so skipping that part would be a bit brainless, too.

HEARTY STEW
Innards for the Anti-vivisectionist

1-1/2 lbs green cabbage
2 heaping Tbs Chinese or other dried mushrooms
2 Tbs butter
3 cups Bumstock II
1 large celery heart, quartered
1 Tbs sesame oil
1 Tbs soy sauce
1 Tbs Insta-Steer II
2 Tbs dry Sherry
Vegebutcher salt to taste

1. Remove outer leaves of cabbage and reserve for use in another dish (or as a Bum Wrap; see MOCKING UP). Cut heart in quarters. Soak mushrooms in hot water for 20 mins and remove stems.

2. Preheat oven to 325°. Heat butter in casserole and saute mushrooms and cabbage hearts for 5 mins. Add broth, soy sauce and Insta-Steer II, and seasonings. Bring to a boil, place casserole in oven and bake for 30 mins.

3. Briefly saute celery in sesame oil and add to stew along with sherry and any additional salt and pepper that seems called for. Bake 15 mins more.

4. Serve spooned-out over a platter of toast hearts (you can make them with heart-shaped cutters and soft bread) and of course, serve the remaining stew juices in a ceramic cow creamer.

> The French eat more meat than any other Europeans, averaging 189 pounds per person in 1972. The Germans, in second place, averaged 166 pounds. The Germans led the pork-eating field with an average consumption of 82 lbs.
> — *New York Times*, Dec. 8, 1974

"BREADS"
4 ounces of fresh unsweetened coconut meat
1 cup of prepared Gluten
1 egg

SAUCE
1 Tbs each: fresh lemon juice, dark brown sugar, crushed garlic
1 tsp each: Vegebutcher salt, Mock MSG I, powdered coriander, powdered
    curry, red pepper flakes or chili pepper
1 Tbs sesame (or peanut) oil
1 cup water
1/4 cup Mock-Chicken Marinade

   1. Combine the water and marinade with the coconut meat and simmer, stirring frequently, until coconut is quite soft (20 mins certainly). Put coconut meat into a ricer or press through a sieve. Reserve juices.
   2. Put coconut meat and Gluten through meat grinder and combine in mixing bowl with egg, slightly whipped. Shape into small balls and put into a steamer with boiling water below. Steam-cook for 15 mins.
   3. Meanwhile, saute remaining ingredients in sesame oil until soft and pour on reserved coconut-marinade juices. Stir and heat til warm. Put "sweet breads" in a casserole, cover with these juices and bake about 20 mins at 350° (sauce will thicken during baking) . . . serve with a platter of pasta (bow-tie macaroni? buttered fusilli? . . .).

In the opinion of many experts, meat-eating is a form of malnutrition, and the rise in meat consumption (Americans now consume 250 lbs. apiece each year compared to the 50 lbs. eaten by the Japanese) may indeed be linked with the rise in heart disease . . .

THE VEGE-DELI

COWLESS COLD CUTS

1 cup tomato puree, 1 cup water or Bumstock II
1 cup toasted peanuts
2 Tbs gluten flour
1-1/4 cups finely chopped peanuts
1-1/4 cups soy granules or soy flour
2 Tbs onion flakes
1 minced crushed clove garlic
1 tsp Vegebutcher salt
2 Tbs soy sauce

1. Puree first 3 ingredients in blender, put in mixing bowl.
2. Thoroughly puree the remaining ingredients and combine in bowl with first mixture.
3. Spoon this coldcut-batter into clean greased 1 lb-coffee cans and fill 2/3 full. Cover top with foil and secure with rubber bands.
4. Steam in a deep kettle of boiling water (it should cover 2/3 of sides of cans) for 2-3 hours until firm (be sure you set cans on a rack inside kettle).
5. Let cans cool slightly, then loosen with a small rubber spatula, turn out and let cool completely.
6. Slice carefully into thickish coldcuts. How about serving them between slices of homemade steamed brown bread?

PHONEY BALONEY
Hot or Cold

1 lb chick-pea flour
1-1/2 qts water
1 Tbs freshly chopped parsley
1 tsp ground mustard seed
1 tsp Vegebutcher salt
1/2 tsp butter flavor extract or 1 tsp miso

    1. Put everything except flour into kettle.
    2. Heat over a slow burner until lukewarm.
    3. Gradually stir in flour while pot is still over burner. Introduce slowly with a continuous motion, being sure to spoon bottom to prevent lumpiness.
    4. Continue stirring until flour begins to thicken and to separate from kettle.
    5. Immediately put into glass containers to mold (freezer Mason jars, 1/2 pt or 1 pt size are fine). Chill.
    6. Remove from jars (with rubber spatula) and slice thin baloney rounds.
    7. Dredge in vegetable oil or soy butter and bake 25 mins til golden brown in a 325° oven. Serve hot, or refrigerate and use like coldcuts. With either style, a helping of herbed cabbage (see ON THE SIDE) wouldn't hurt.

LIVER-LESS LIVERWURST

1 large egg
1/2 lb very fresh raw mushrooms
1 cup olive oil
1/2 tsp miso or marmite
1/2 tsp Vegebutcher salt
1/2 tsp poultry seasoning
1/4 tsp pepper

    1. All ingredients should be at room temperature. Put egg in blender container with 1/4 cup of oil and blend on "chop" for 10 seconds.

2. Add miso or marmite, salt, pepper, poultry seasoning and, with blender running on "chop", gradually and steadily, in a stream, add the remaining oil til it is all blended. Turn blender to "liquefy" for a few seconds.

3. Chop mushrooms (do not wash) and with blender on "puree" add them to the above mixture, a handful at a time, until they are incorporated and mixture is a smooth puree.

4. Chill thoroughly, correct seasoning, serve as sandwich or cracker spread

SURROGATE SALAMI
More Nein Swine Niceties

2 cups bean pulp (residue from making Tofu)
1 cup whole-wheat flour
1 cup corn meal flour
1 small egg
1/4 cup vegetable oil
1 tsp Vegebutcher salt
1 tsp sage
1 tsp thyme
1 tsp oregano
1/2 tsp allspice
1/2 tsp black pepper
1/2 tsp crushed red pepper
1 tsp garlic flakes
1 tsp onion flakes

1. Combine squeezed pulp with everything else and mix well (the mixture will be moist but should be considerably drier than a batter).

2. Remove ends from a 2-lb coffee can (save them), grease the can very generously and pack in the "sausage" mixture. Wrap each end with foil to secure.

3. Bake in a 350° oven for 1 hour, or 30 mins more if unsure. Cool slightly, and use a reserved can-end to gently push loaf out of can. Cool completely (you can do this in the refrigerator).

4. When cooled, slice as thinly as possible and saute in garlic-flavored olive oil until browned on both sides. Best while warm and buttery between toasted rye bread slices.

MOCK MINUTE-STEAKS

4 prepared Gluten steaks
1 Tbs soaked garlic flakes
1 tsp prepared mustard
1 Tbs orange marmalade
sea salt
pinch thyme

1. Sprinkle the towel-dried steaks with seasonings.
2. Spread with mustard, then marmalade. Run under preheated broiler for about 10 mins.
3. Serve on toast or atop an Underbum (see ON THE SIDE) or with the potatoes below.

MOCK MINUTE-SPUDS

Cut lengthwise strips, 1/2'' to 1/8'' thick, from washed and dried mock spuds (jerusalem artichokes). Place on greased baking sheet, sprinkle with Vege-butcher salt or Homemade Poultry Seasoning and paprika. Bake at 500° for a few mins until potatoes puff up.

Note: You may use real baking potatoes or sweet potatoes instead of the mock spuds.

BEEF-FREE "BEEF" JERKY
A Tomato Leather for Meat-totalers

upwards of 5 lbs of ripe Beefsteak tomatoes
1 cup sugar and 1 Tbs salt for each gallon of tomato pulp
upwards of 10 cups of boiling water

hardware: platters or baking sheets, upwards of 3 yards of butcher paper or clean brown packaging paper, canner or kettle of similar capaciousness

1. Pour boiling water to cover tomatoes and when cooled, peel them.
2. Put pulp into a heavy canner or kettle and cook briskly until reduced by half.
3. For each gallon pulp, mix in 1 cup sugar and 1 Tbs salt.
4. Spread the mixture on platters or cookie sheets (the latter if you prefer to do your drying in the oven indoors) and dry in the full sun and fresh air for about a fortnight.
5. Store in layers with paper between.

BURGER BITS
Teriyaki Tofu Snacks

2 Tbs dry sherry
2 tsp cornstarch
1/3 cup soy sauce
2 cloves minced garlic
2 Tbs brown sugar or date sugar plus 2 Tbs honey
1/2 tsp ground ginger
1/4 tsp dry mustard
1 lb Tofu cut into burger bits
3 Tbs toasted sesame seeds

1. Combine sherry and cornstarch in small saucepan.
2. Stir in all but last 2 ingredients and cook, stirring until mixture thickens. Cool.
3. Pour mixture over Tofu bits, cover pan and marinate 1 hour.
4. Carefully lift Tofu from sauce and place on greased rack in broiler pan. Broil 3'' from heat (basting before and once during cooking) about 1 min on each side. Sprinkle with sesame seed. Serve hot. Add rice and buttered sprouted peas for a complete Dimsum, or as is, on picks, for party snacks.

6 green (sometimes yellow) frying peppers about the length and shape of
    frankfurters
1 cup of soft drained cottage-type cheese (ricotta may be used)
1 cup of roughly grated spiced Mexican cheese (second choice: a sharp cheddar)
6 medium eggs
cumin salt
6 Tbs hot water
enough flour to make a thin batter

    1. Briefly steam-cook the peppers (do 3 at a time in a large covered saucepot with a spare amount of water, or use your steamer) until they are softened but not limp. Cool and remove the seeds by slitting lengthwise, almost but not quite, from end to end.
    2. Cream the soft cheese and incorporate the grated cheese.
    3. Stuff the chilis and fasten with toothpicks. If necessary, they may also be laced with thread to further secure the filling.
    4. Beat eggs to a froth, add cumin salt (grind 1 tsp of whole cumin, then regrind with 2 Tbs salt), water and about 1/2 cup flour. Dip each chili-dog in batter and deep fry until golden brown. Drain on paper toweling. Eat with hot mustard or mild mayonnaise spiked with more of the hand-crafted Mexican salt above. Tuck into a hot-dog roll or less conventionally (and less fatteningly) into large, cold, crisp leaves of spinach, romaine, butter or iceberg lettuce and serve with Phoney Peanuts (see ON THE SIDE).

> Hot dogs not labelled "All Meat" in fact usually contain only 2.5% less actual meat than hot dogs so labelled, according to a lower-court decision affirmed by the District of Columbia Court of Appeals.

THE BUN
4 cups whole-wheat flour
1/4 cup vegetable oil and 1/4 cup melted butter or soy butter
1 cup Bumstock II or water

1. Blend half the oil-butter mixture with flour.
2. Blend in liquid gradually and knead dough until smooth on a lightly floured surface.
3. Let dough rest, lightly covered, for half an hour.
4. Divide dough into 24 equal pieces. Roll each one into a 5″ round.
5. Brush with remaining oil-butter and fold in half, brush again and fold again. Roll out round again until somewhat oblong in shape. Dust lightly with flour and spread with filling (below) to within 1/4″ of edges. Roll to achieve a cigar or hot-dog shape, and pinch ends to seal.
6. Put Underdogs on greased cookie sheet, brush with oil-butter and slash each one (as you do broiled franks) three times. Sprinkle with paprika.
7. Bake in a preheated 375° oven for 10 mins, turn and bake about 7 mins on opposite side. Serve with Cow-Cow Chow Chow (see ON THE SIDE), or cole slaw.

THE FILLING
Saute 2 cups Grainola or Seedmeat in 2 Tbs vegetable oil with 1 finely chopped onion, and 1 tsp each ground cumin, ground coriander, salt and chili powder and 1/4 tsp pepper. When well heated and soft, set aside til cool. Stuff or spread as directed.

HERBIVORE'S HEAD-CHEESE

1 envelope plain gelatin
3/4 cup water
1 tsp Vegebutcher salt
1/4 tsp mixed pickling spices, ground
1/4 tsp ground pepper
3/4 cup cottage cheese plus 3 Tbs water
1-1/2 cups raw chopped spinach
4 Tbs lemon juice
4 hard-cooked eggs, chopped

1. Sprinkle gelatin over 3/4 cup cold water in saucepan. Place over low heat and stir constantly about 4 mins until gelatin dissolves. Remove from heat, stir in salt, spices and pepper. Chill, stirring off and on, until mixture has consistency of unbeaten egg white.
2. Put cottage cheese and 3 Tbs water in blender, cover and process at high speed until smooth. Add spinach, lemon juice, cottage cheese and diced egg to gelatin. Mix well.
3. Pour into 3 qt-capacity rectangular mold or loaf pan. Chill until firm. Unmold and slice for sandwiches, crackers or entree for a summer supper.

"In its unhulled form, the sesame seed contains more calcium than cow's milk, one-and-a-half times more iron than beef liver, three times more phosphorus than eggs, and more *protein than chicken, beef liver or beefsteak.*"
— Ann Wigmore,
Hippocrates Health Institute, Boston, Mass.

BUMSTEADS
Two Burgers for Meat-totalers

I

2 Tbs peanut, soy or olive oil
2 Tbs minced onion or shallot
2 Tbs chopped celery
1 cup cooked brown rice (or 1 cup Grainola)
1 cup mashed Tofu
1 cup sprouted peas or beans (the smaller the better) roughly chopped (leave
    whole if *very* small)
1/2 cup Bum Crumbs or whole-wheat crumbs
1 Tbs soy sauce or Insta-Steer Savory
1/2 tsp Vegebutcher salt

    1. Saute onion and celery until lightly browned.
    2. Combine with all other ingredients and shape into patties. Roll in additional Bum Crumbs or breadcrumbs.
    3. Place on oiled cookie sheet and turn patties to grease opposite side. Bake in 350° oven for 20 mins. Good on a sesame seed bun with Soybean Mustard (see THE MOCK CROCK).

II

1 cup Gluten
1 beaten egg and 1 Tbs onion flakes
4 or more Tbs potato starch
2 tsp Vegebutcher salt
1 Tbs soy sauce

    1. Put the Gluten through meat grinder, then into a bowl.
    2. Add remaining ingredients and shape into patties (adding additional potato flour if necessary).
    3. Saute in greased skillet until brown, turn over, saute again; sprinkle with soy sauce and steam briefly to bring out flavors (5 mins covered). Yummy on onion rolls with fresh grated radish.

BUMSTEAD JUNIOR
Meatless Microcosmics

1 cup sifted whole-wheat or triticale flour
1/2 cup chopped sunflower or lentil sprouts
1 egg, separated
freshly ground fines herbes, Vegebutcher salt, freshly ground pepper, fresh
    chopped dill weed, to taste
diluted miso or soy sauce for dipping

1. Sift flour and stir in sprouts and seasonings.
2. Beat egg white til nearly stiff.
3. Combine yolk with small amount of milk and stir into dry ingredients.
Fold in egg white and add any additional flour or milk necessary to shape very
small (walnut-sized) balls, light and soft, but not sticky.
4. Drop into a kettle of busily simmering broth and simmer gently about 6
mins. Balls will double in size during cooking.
5. Drain and fold up inside a floppy oven-warmed tortilla or tuck 2 or 3 into
a conventional hot-dog bun. If you don't want to tuck them into anything other
than your mouth, stick them with toothpicks and pass with a simple dipping
sauce: just soy sauce or diluted miso. Serve with Mock Popped Corn (see ON
THE SIDE).

BUMSTICKS
Beef-free Brochette-free Bread-free Finger Sandwiches

4 large cabbage or Chinese cabbage leaves, steamed and cooled
2 medium-sized avocados, diced
1 medium-sized tomato, diced
2 green onions
garlic powder, kelp, oregano, cayenne pepper and Vegebutcher salt to taste
mayonnaise or nut butter

1. Mash avocado, add chopped onion, tomato and seasonings. Mix well.
2. Spread each leaf with mayonnaise (or Mock Mayonnaise) or nut butter
and spread again with avocado mixture.

3. Roll leaf and eat (as you would a taco) then and there or later, after a decent cooling-off period.

Note: The avocado provides more energy, pound for pound, than almost any other food. It's as digestible as milk, a good source of high quality protein and respectable amounts of vitamins A, B, C, D, and E, plus unsaturated fruit fat (the avocado is 16% oil) for which a low-fat dieter can be thankful (he has now discovered what a perfect butter replacement avocado is).

BREAKFAST SQUARES

1/2 cup boiled or steamed sweet potato (or yam)
6 Tbs vegetable oil
1/2 cup oatmeal ground in blender
1 cup whole-wheat flour
pinch of salt
1 Tbs lemon juice
2 Tbs honey
pinch of mace

1. Put potato in blender with lemon juice (to prevent discoloring of potato pulp), oil, honey. Puree.
2. Put into bowl with remaining ingredients and knead with fingers, adding more flour if necessary to get a very soft but not sticky dough.
3. Press dough into a large square baking dish or square griddle or skillet and cut into squares.
4. Bake squares in 400° oven for about 15 mins until done through and browned. Delicious with Pigless Pork Sausage.

HUM BUMS ON HUM BUNS
A Sort of Moroccan Burger with Homemade Pocket Bread

Prepare Hummus (recipe follows) and mash the puree with the following:
2 to 4 Tbs sesame tahini or finely ground toasted sesame
2 large peeled and pressed garlic cloves
1 cup medium-coarse whole-wheat or whole-grain bread crumbs
juice of 1 large lemon
vegetable oil
cornstarch, paprika, wheat germ
salt and pepper (or kelp and sea salt) to taste

1. Combine in a bowl and mix well. Add more crumbs if mixture is still too moist.
2. Chill, then shape into oblong burgerish "Hum Bums" and dredge in cornstarch-paprika-wheat germ breading and brown in well-heated vegetable oil in an iron skillet til browned and crisp on both sides.
3. Drain and tuck into middle of a Hum Bun (see below). Garnish with fresh watercress sprigs or something shredded that's in season.

HUM BUNS
1. Put 2 cups of warm water into bowl and sprinkle with 1 Tbs yeast.
2. Add 1 tsp salt and slowly stir in 2 cups unbleached white flour and 2-1/2 cups whole-wheat flour. Beat til smooth, cover bowl and let rise til doubled in bulk.
3. Punch dough down and divide into a dozen equal parts. Arrange on a floured board and let stand 30 mins.
4. Oil a large cookie sheet and place only a few buns at a time on sheet. Lightly press around edges to force air bubbles into center of bread, creating "pocket."
5. Place sheet on lowest rack of oven and bake at 350° for 20 mins. Hum Buns should appear puffy but pale.
6. When entire batch has been baked, place them under broiler for a quick top-browning. For sandwiches: slit open the edge of a bun a third of the way around and insert filling. These breads (use them warm or cooled) will keep up to a week, but no more.

134

SPREADS
Hummus

2 cups cooked chick-peas
1/4 cup cooking liquid or vegetable broth
1/4 cup lemon juice
2 tsp chopped garlic
3 Tbs sesame tahini (below)
2 Tbs olive oil
2 Tbs chopped parsley
1 tsp Vegebutcher salt

1. Puree chick-peas and liquid. Blend in lemon juice, garlic and salt. Add tahini and mash mixture until smooth.
2. Put Hummus in a flat soup plate, sprinkle parsley on top and, if desired, pour oil over surface just before serving. Refrigerate and use in any all-purposeful ways that occur to you in hungry moments.

Sesame Tahini

1-1/2 Tbs lime juice
1 tsp oil
1 tsp kelp
6 Tbs water
1/2 cup finely ground sesame seeds

1. Put everything but seeds in blender container. Gradually add the seeds, processing until mixture is smooth and creamy. Refrigerate. Use as suggested in recipes. Good cracker snack, good salad dressing.

Cold Turkey

Mix 1/4 cup each: unsalted pecans and almonds into one pound of Tofu (or storebought cottage cheese). Blender-chop this mixture until it becomes a thick-ish puree. Add 1 tsp each chopped onion, pimento, green pepper, and season with powdered celery, sage and 1/2 tsp horseradish. Mold into a loaf pan. Chill. Serve sliced or spread on sliced bread.

135

Cold Tuna

Put the following in your blender jar: 1/2 cup toasted, finely ground hulled sesame seeds, 1 tsp kelp powder, 1 cup Bumstock I (failing that, water), 1/2 chopped onion and 1/2 rib of celery, 1/2 cup of mixed mung, lentil, alfalfa sprouts, 2 tsp mild vegetable oil, 2 tsp Vegebutcher salt. Process and chill. A good celery filling; a better breadspread.

Cold Chicken

Grind 2 cups chopped cauliflower heads with 1 green onion, 1 cup chopped celery. Add 1 tsp sesame butter, 2 tsp Vegebutcher salt, 3 tsp Homemade Poultry Seasoning, 1/4 cup almond nut butter. Spread on cold nut bread.

Mock Lox

3 carrots, scraped and finely chopped
1/2 cup unsalted cashew nuts
1 Tbs peanut or cashew butter
1 Tbs plain yogurt
1 tsp sea water (a pinch of sea salt or kelp in tap or mineral water)
1/2 tsp dill weed
1/2 tsp hickory-smoked salt

　　1. Combine nut butter, yogurt, water, dill and salt in jar of blender. Process until smooth and put 3/4 of the mixture in a small bowl.
　　2. Add chopped carrots and cashews to blender and process with remaining mixture until smooth and pasty. Good on homemade celery-seed crackers (substitute celery seeds in your favorite sesame-seed cracker recipe) or sticks of fresh raw anise. Or, serve as an appetizer pate pressed into clam shells.

Mock Lobster

1 cup finely grated carrots
1 cup very finely shredded parsnips
1/2 cup well-chopped walnuts
1/2 tsp horseradish sauce (or more according to taste)
1/4 tsp crushed fennel seed
mock sour cream as needed

1. Combine carrot and parsnip shreddings. Add the rest, combining well. Make mock sour cream by pureeing cottage cheese in blender til curds are no more.
2. Chill. Spread on squares of warm hardtack and pass the lobster bibs.

A new contaminant has appeared in fish caught in Michigan waters. The bromine compound, a fire retardant called PBB, causes liver and kidney damage at levels as low as two parts per million, according to Michigan Chemical Company vice president for Research and Development, Dr. A. Fred Kerst. Levels of more than one part per million are not allowed in beef or milk for human consumption. There are no safety levels set for PBB in fish thus far, according to the State Agriculture Dept.

MOCKING UP: GENERAL DISHES

GREENBUTCHER'S QUICHE

pate brisee (or your favorite rich pastry shell)
3-1/2 cups chopped watercress
1 Tbs butter
1 tsp nut butter with 1 tsp Homemade Poultry Seasoning
6 poached eggs
1-1/2 cups bechamel sauce (or another more favored sauce. See THE MOCK
    CROCK for a selection)
1/3 cup freshly grated parmesan cheese

1. Roll out prepared pastry dough 1/8'' thick on lightly floured surface. Drape dough over rolling pin and fit into 9'' flan pan with removable fluted ring. Press dough firmly into pan and cut off any excess with floured rolling pin. Prick bottom of shell with fork and chill shell for 1 hour.

2. Line shell with wax paper, fill paper with rice (just for weight) and bake shell in lower third of preheated 400° oven for 10 mins. Carefully remove paper and rice (save it for some other recipe) and bake shell 10-15 mins more until lightly browned.

3. Remove shell from tin, transfer to rack and let cool.

4. Saute watercress in butter for 3 mins and stir in nut butter and seasoning. Return shell to tin and spread watercress mixture inside. Top with poached eggs and spoon bechamel sauce into shell.

5. Sprinkle quiche with cheese and broil under preheated broiler for 5 mins or until nicely browned.

1 cup cooked horse beans (fava beans)
1 cup sprouted horse beans (you may substitute sprouted marrow beans) or 1 cup
    Seedmeat
1 tsp bottled horseradish or 2 tsp fresh grated horseradish
1 tsp each, Vegebutcher salt and Insta-Steer Savory or Starter II
1 cup steamed hulled oats or barley
1 large egg
1/4 cup whole-wheat bread crumbs or soy grits
1/4 cup tomato juice or vegetable broth

    1. Put juice or broth in blender with cooked horse beans (favas should be soaked overnight and then cooked 1 hour the following day. You may eat them pod and all if not too mature. Otherwise, shell like green peas), puree.
    2. Put puree in mixing bowl with sprouts and everything else.
    3. Combine the whole horsy works well, using fingers.
    4. Press into a well-greased horseshoe mold (or a loaf pan) and bake at 325° about 45 mins, or divide up and bake 4 small "babas" instead (use baba-form pan).
    5. Unmold and serve with Oat Gravy or Horseless Horseradish (see THE MOCK CROCK).

Note: The somewhat neglected horsebean is 25% protein and is the nutritional equal of the wheat berry. This is not to suggest that you switch to Cream of Horse, but there are worse things you could put in your breakfast feedbag.

CHERRY BERRY BUM
A Frugivore's Pilaf

2 cups long-grain rice
3 medium onions
1/4 cup oil or butter
2 tsp coriander, ground
1 tsp Mock MSG I
1 cup pan-roasted whole-wheat berries
enough Bumstock II to cover mixture by 1''
chopped parsley
1/2 cup or more pitted, cooked and drained cherries
Vegebutcher salt to taste
1 Tbs oil

   1. Wash and drain rice several times until water runs clear.
   2. Towel-dry rice and set aside. Heat oil in a heavy casserole with lid and saute onion, sliced, until tender. Stir in rice and spices. Cook mixture, stirring, over medium heat until rice is glossy and transparent.
   3. In a separate skillet, put 1 Tbs oil and toast-saute wheat berries, tossing them around skillet with wooden spatula, until lightly brown and toasty-smelling.
   4. Stir berries into rice mixture, add salt to taste and Bumstock. Bring mixture to a boil, cover tightly, finish cooking in a preheated 350° oven for 20 mins.
   5. When all stock is absorbed, stir in cherries and chopped parsley. Serve with some braised dove-like endive on the side.

MEATLESS MINCEMEAT
For Use in Pies, Pastries or As Pressed "Meat" Loaf

1 cup cubed, cooked Tofu
1 cup prepared ground, or minced, Gluten
4 cups chopped raw apple
1/2 cup chopped citron
3 cups raisins or currants
1 cup chopped apricots (or dried bananas or other dried fruit)
1 cup date sugar or brown sugar
3/4 cup molasses
1-1/2 cups sweet cider
1/2 cup soy butter plus 1/4 cup lecithin granules and 1/4 cup vegetable oil
1/2 cup cereal coffee (such as Postum)
1/2 cup Bumstock II or vegetable broth
1/2 cup mixed citrus peel (lemon, orange, tangerine, grapefruit, kumquat, lime, or any combination thereof)
1 tsp each: ground nutmeg, ground cloves, Vegebutcher salt, cinnamon, allspice

1. Saute mockmeats (first 2 ingredients) in butter and oil.
2. Add lecithin and mix in all remaining ingredients (except liquids) by hand (let your fingers do the mixing), combining everything *thoroughly*.
3. Put in a big saucepot or canner with liquids and steam slowly for an hour or more.
4. Divide up and store in jars. Should keep nicely in a very cool place or in a second refrigerator (or freeze half for future pies and pastries).

> Ironically enough, the word meat means food. Yet meat is a very poor source of minerals, especially magnesium, the very mineral which is needed to handle the large amounts of protein in flesh foods.

GOLDEN BUCK
1 lb grated sharp cheddar cheese
2 Tbs heavy cream or thick yogurt
1/2 cup stale ale (or flat gingerbeer)
Vegebutcher salt to taste
1/2 tsp grated nutmeg
1 tsp miso or Worcestershire sauce
2 eggs lightly beaten
freshly grated black pepper
4 poached eggs

    1. Combine cheese, cream and ale in a heavy saucepan or chafing dish. Cook, stirring, until cheese is melted.
    2. Add miso and spices.
    3. Reduce heat and stir in eggs, beating constantly with a wire whisk.
    4. When thick and creamy, spoon in equal portions over some sort of Underbum or buttered buckwheat bread. Serve with Fritter Critters (see ON THE SIDE).

ENGLISH MONKEY
1/2 cup stale bread crumbs, or Bum Crumbs
1 cup milk or Mock Milk
Vegebutcher salt
1 well-beaten egg
cayenne
dry mustard
1/2 cup monkey nuts (peanuts), toasted but not salted.

    1. Soak crumbs in milk for 15 mins.
    2. Melt butter in a heavy enamel saucepan and add cheese.
    3. Stir until cheese melts.
    4. Add egg to crumbs and milk mixture and stir in seasonings. Add to cheese mixture along with nuts. Stir til very smooth.
    5. Spoon out over monkey nut bread or soft biscuits.

143

RED FLANNEL HASH
A Classic, Beefed Down

1 Tbs butter or sesame oil
1/4 cup of dried apricots chopped into small dice
3/4 cup fairly dry, cooked (steamed) kasha or bulgur
3 cups chopped boiled potatoes
1 cup chopped cooked beets
1/2 cup chopped onion
1/2 tsp MSG II, or 1/2 tsp poultry seasoning
1/8 tsp freshly ground pepper

1. Combine kasha and potatoes, moistening with a small amount of additional oil if necessary.
2. Add beets, onion and seasoning and mix well. Heat oil or butter in a heavy skillet until bubbles have subsided, then spread mixture evenly in the pan and brown slowly until crust forms on bottom.
3. Turn as you would an omelet, brown the bottom side and turn onto a hot platter. Cut into wedges and serve to four famished frugivores. Garnish with watercress and sprout salad, plus just-baked fruit bread.

BUM WRAPS
To Be Served at Room Temperature

I *(with leaves)*
Into the midsection of just slightly steam-wilted and very large chard leaves, put the following stuffing:
Saute in a skillet 1 cup minced onion, 1/3 cup minced celery, 2 Tbs minced parsley, and 1 tsp thyme in 1/4 cup dairy or mock butter until vegetables are softened. Add 3/4 cup seeded, halved grapes, 1/2 cup vegetable broth and 1/4 cup raisins. Bring to a boil, add 4 cups toasted bread cubes, and season with salt to taste.

II *(with leaves again)*

Into the center of just slightly steam-wilted, very fresh and large savoy cabbage leaves put the following stuffing:

   1/2 cup chopped onion sauteed in 1-1/2 Tbs olive oil (for a meaty flavor), mixed with 2 cups cooked wild rice, 1 slightly beaten egg and 1 tsp oregano powder. Saute everything a second time, cool slightly before stuffing. Very deluxe lukewarm, but still classy fare cold.

III *(with seaweed)*

Quick-dip one sheet of nori (for bath water use stock, sherry, or plain tap water) and wrap up a scooperful of Hash, Bum Stir, or anything else that seems glorious and omnivorious today. Wrap tight and steam-cook (no pre-greasing necessary) 15 mins.

IV *(with egg-roll skins)*

Egg-roll skins or won ton wrappers or spring roll skins, all economically available at oriental food stores, are ready to wrap around anything and deep fry. Bring them to room temperature first.

V *(with parchment paper)*

Cut paper into suitable-sized squares. Minced meat stuffings, for instance, require nothing more than a 6″ x 6″ sheet, as would a pate mix. Less processed fillings like Burger Bits will need perhaps a 7″ x 9″ cut-out. Marinate prepared Gluten pieces (see recipes in VEGEBUTCHERING) and Tofu chunks first. Cooked bean mixtures may simply be enclosed and cooked. Use an envelope or diaper-fold and place packages seam sides down on baking sheet in a 350° oven (you may insert a slice of lime or lemon or fresh ginger on top of filling before closing). Open at table, one to a customer.

Fridge Finger-food-making Note: You may carry this eating exercise one step further and refrigerate the stuffed Wraps. Later, slice into thirds and serve on small lace doilies to your guests or yourself or whoever is around to be grateful for such offerings after hours. Good with mayonnaise, of course.

PET CHOW
Basic Dry Form

1 cup dried brewer's yeast
1 cup wheat or corn germ
1 cup fine bone meal
1 cup dried sea greens

Keep dry and covered in a glass jar or coffee can. To serve, moisten with broth or milk and extend with an extra cup of crumbled whole-wheat bread, whole-grain crackers or cooked grain. Occasionally, beef up with egg whipped with yogurt.

Basic Wet Form

1 bunch celery
1 lb oatmeal, or whole-wheat, or rye berries
1 large onion and 1 clove garlic
3 qts water and salt
2 cups Tofu pulp
1 bunch carrots

Chop vegetables fine and mix with whole-wheat or oats. Put in kettle and cover with water. Boil and then reduce to a simmer. Simmer 1 hour, add salt and stir in Tofu pulp (the unused pulp from making Tofu). If you have none, substitute cottage cheese or farmer's cheese. Consistency should be stew-like. Store in glass jars and refrigerate.

"We pay at least five cents more a pound for meat because of the pet food industry", says USDA economist George Allen; "Pet food companies have been stealing our precious cattle feed by outbidding the farmers and driving up the price of feed grain."
— *Let's Live* Magazine, Dec., 1974

1/2 cup wheat flakes*
1/2 cup cracked wheat or bulgur
1/2 cup raw oatmeal
1 cup vegetable broth
3 medium-sized raw carrots, roughly chopped
1 egg
2 Tbs bonemeal or milk powder
1/4 cup soy granules or grits
1/2 bunch parsley
1 medium boiling onion, quartered
undegerminated corn meal as needed

1. Put carrots, onion, parsley through food grinder
2. Meanwhile soak oatmeal, cracked wheat and wheat flakes in vegetable broth for 15 mins.
3. Combine soaked grains, ground vegetables and remaining ingredients in a mixing bowl. Combine thoroughly.
4. If loaf seems a bit "wet," correct with addition of corn meal.
5. Put loaf into a greased and lightly dusted (with corn meal) loaf pan and bake in a 350° oven for 30 mins. When cool, transfer by chunks to a jar or canister. Keep refrigerated.

Makes 5-6 half-cup servings or 12 good portions if used as meat-extender for canned dog food. Preparation time: 20 mins plus 30 mins baking time. Cost: less than 10 cents per half-cup serving.

*Unsugared, unsalted, natural whole-wheat flakes are available in any well-stocked natural-foods store.

MUSH PUPPY
A Quick Complete-protein Canine Cereal That's Ready in 15 Minutes.

1/2 cup dried lentils
1/2 cup dried green (split) peas
1/2 cup soy granules or soy grits
5 Tbs nutritional (brewer's) yeast
5 Tbs dry milk powder
1/4 cup each: garlic flakes and onion flakes
2 Tbs raw wheat germ or raw oatmeal
1 Tbs powdered seaweed (kelp or dulse) optional

    1. Blender-grind lentils and peas until you have a meal-like consistency. Put into a large mixing bowl and stir in remaining ingredients.

    2. Store in a large-mouthed jar, or tightly capped coffee can, on cupboard shelf.

    3. To re-constitute: 4 heaping Tbs to 2 cups water. Bring to boil, simmer 10 mins, let cool 5.

Note: Makes almost 2-1/2 cups dry mush powder, or about 80 puppy portions. Preparation Time: 15 mins plus 15 mins cooking time. Cost: Less than 2¢ per serving.

3/4 to 1 lb green beans
boiling water
2 Tbs crude unrefined vegetable oil such as soy or peanut. (Sold by Walnut Acres and other mail-order natural food suppliers. Its taste is a bit strong for most human palates, but it is very, very nutritious.)
1 chopped onion
1 large garlic clove, pressed and chopped
1 large hard-cooked egg
1 Tbs powdered kelp (or use 1 tsp salt if you haven't any of this seaweed, available in small shakers at health food stores.)
1 Tbs food (brewer's) yeast (optional)

1. Trim beans and cook, covered, in small amount of boiling water, until tender (about 20 mins).
2. Heat oil and brown onion and garlic lightly.
3. Drain beans and chop finely or grind.
4. Mash egg with beans, blend in onion, garlic and kelp (or salt) and yeast to form a compact mass. Chill and store in refrigerator.

> "The American dog may consume 275 lbs. a year of 'Semi-Moist Burger Patties' or 'Burgers 'n Cheese Dinner.' The meat consumed comes from five times the dogs own weight in grain . . . so that a dog actually eats enough food for two adult humans living on a nutritionally complete grain diet . . ."
> — *New York Times* (letters), Oct. 29, 1974

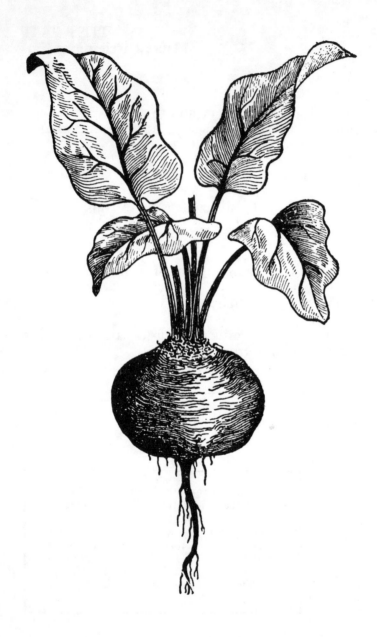

THE MOCK CROCK

VEGETABLE VEGETARIAN SOUP
With Or Without Mock Oxtails

1/2 lb fresh okra (if canned, drain and add during final five mins)
2 large onions and 2 green peppers, chopped
1 large minced garlic clove
1 eggplant, peeled and chopped into cubes
4 peeled, seeded and chopped tomatoes
1 cup Bumstock II or vegetable broth
1 bay leaf
1/8 tsp cayenne
2 Tbs vegetable oil
1 cup tomato juice
Vegebutcher salt to taste
For Oxtails: 1 large lotus root*

    1. In soup kettle, saute okra, onions, peppers, garlic, until soft, in vegetable oil. Add everything else, bring to a boil, lower heat and simmer one hour.

    2. With Oxtails: Scrub and slice lotus root into 1/2''-thick slices. Stuff, or not, with partially-cooked rice and add to soup with all the other ingredients.

*Lotus Root, available in Oriental foodstores, is a highly versatile fruit-vegetable which resembles the fine blade of a food grinder when it is sliced. When stuffed, it bears a mocking resemblance to oxtails. An ingredient worth the searching after.

2-1/2 qts water, part of which may be vegetable broth or Bumstock I
2 cups turtle beans
3/4 cup olive oil
3 chopped onions
4 cloves minced garlic
1 tsp hickory-smoked salt, optional
1 Tbs dry sherry
2 bay leaves
2 green peppers
Vegebutcher salt, to taste

1. Bring stock to a boil and stir in beans and bay leaves. Cook til beans are almost tender.

2. Heat olive oil (the large amount of oil here accounts for the luscious end results, so don't skimp) and cook onion, peppers, garlic til nearly tender. Add these to bean-pot and simmer away til everything is tender. Remove from heat and let stand overnight to blend flavors. Add sherry just before reheating.

3. Serve with steamed rice and a Fritter Critter from the selection in ON THE SIDE; or serve, most appropriately, with turtle shells (seeded and halved avocados) — one half per one whole person.

> "Enough protein is lost through the process of eating meat and poultry — about 18 million tons — to make up 90% of the protein deficit in the entire world . . ."
> — Frances Moore Lappe, *Diet for a Small Planet*, Ballantine Books, 1971

BONELESS MARROW SOUP
A Beefed-down, Beaned-up Soup Bowl

1 cup dried marrow beans (butter beans may be substituted)
4 cups water
7 cups of fresh cabbage cut into 1/2'' slices
4 cups sliced mushrooms
3 cups sliced fennel
2 cups chopped onion
1/2 cup vegetable oil
6 cups Bumstock II, or 6 cups vegetable broth
1 cup rice or any of the longer-cooking grains
4 eggs
1/3 cup lemon juice

1. Simmer rinsed marrow beans in 4 cups water, covered, for 1 hour, or until beans are tender.

2. Saute cabbage, then mushrooms, fennel and onions in a large heavy skillet (do this in batches) in oil over high heat, stirring for 5 mins.

3. Add beans with their liquid and 6 cups of stock. Bring to a boil, add rice or other grain and simmer 20 mins.

4. In another bowl, beat eggs with lemon juice, add reserved liquid in a stream, beating constantly. Transfer sauce to pan and cook over moderate heat for 5 mins until thickened.

5. Do not boil the soup. Thin, if necessary, with milk or mock milk and serve (to 6-8) with cubed Tofu and chopped fennel leaves. Freezes well.

TWO INSTANT SOUP MIXES
I: Instant Non-chicken Soup Mix

FLAVOR PACKET
1-1/2 oz dried mushrooms
3/4 cup medium barley (dry)
3 Tbs onion flakes or powder
1 tsp turmeric (for chicken-broth color)
1/2 tsp chervil and 1/2 tsp parsley flakes
1 tsp (or more) Vegebutcher salt

    1. At high speed, blender-grind mushrooms for a few seconds. Pour into mixing bowl. Grind barley for 30 seconds or until it looks like coarse sand. Add to the mushrooms.
    2. Measure remaining ingredients into same bowl and stir well until mixture is uniform.
    3. Spoon into large-mouthed jar and store in dark cupboard.
    4. To cook, add 3 Tbs dry powder to 2 cups boiling water or Bumstock I or II, bring to a boil and simmer for 15 mins. Good with cubes of Tofu afloat.

II: Instant Non-beef Soup Mix

FLAVOR PACKET
1/2 cup dried lentils
1/2 cup dried green peas
1/2 cup dried onion flakes
2 Tbs Vegebutcher salt
2 Tbs raw wheat germ
1/4 tsp black pepper
1/4 cup dried dill weed
1 tsp bay-leaf powder
1/4 tsp kelp powder

    1. Blend ingredients in electric blender at medium speed, 1/2 cup at a time, until meal-like. Pour ground ingredients into a large bowl and stir well, mixing until uniform.
    2. Store in an empty peanut-butter jar (or similar container). To serve, mix 3 heaping Tbs to 2 cups water. Bring to boil and simmer 5 mins. Garnish with croutons, chives, whole sprouts.

FOR SOUP

2 cups vegetable broth or Bumstock II
2 cups water
2 tsp Vegebutcher salt
1 thin slice gingeroot
2 eggs
1 Tbs finely shredded scallion or leek
1/2 tsp dry sherry
1/2 tsp Mock MSG II (optional)

1. Mix broth, water, salt, ginger in saucepan.
2. Add seasonings and bring to a boil. Remove ginger.
3. Stir beaten eggs into boiling soup. Remove from heat instantly.
4. Add scallion and cooked Birds Nests.

FOR NESTS

1-1/2 lbs large potatoes
hot oil for frying
cold water

1. Peel potatoes and trim them into large oval shapes, dropping slices in a bowl of cold water as you finish each one.
2. Adjust the fluted blade of a mandoline to 1/4" or use a comparable vegetable slicer and slice each potato giving it a quarter turn after each slice to produce a waffle pattern. Keep slices in cold water until ready to cook.
3. Drain and dry slices well.
4. Heat a 4" double potato-nest basket*in hot deep oil (or use a tea strainer) at 365° for several seconds. Open basket and arrange some larger slices, slightly overlapping, around sides of the larger basket and line bottom with smaller slices. Close basket and fry birds nest until it is golden.
5. Open basket and with point of a knife carefully release potato basket onto paper towels to drain. Finish more birds nests in the same manner. When drained and while still warm, ladle hot soup into deep soup bowls and put one nest in each bowl. For a One-bowl Supper, spoon a poached egg or marinated cubes of Tofu into each nest and sprinkle with chopped coriander, chives, scallion or parsley.

*see STEERAGE for mail ordering information

THREE INSTANT DRINKS
Mock Coffee

Put 1 Tbs blackstrap molasses in a coffee cup. Fill cup with boiling water or warm milk, stir and add a dash of nutmeg, if liked.

The "coffee" here is boiled-down vegetable juice and, of course, totally caffeine-free.

Variation: Put 1/4 tsp ground cardamom in cup along with molasses. Finish as above. Very Christmasy.

Mock Cocoa

Put 1 heaping Tbs vanilla milk powder (milk powder perfumed overnight, or longer, by the addition of half a vanilla bean), 1 heaping Tbs carob powder, 1 tsp honey, and 10 oz water or milk in blender. Process til smooth, pour in saucepan and heat gently.

The "cocoa" here is the product of the Honey Locust Bean dating back to Biblical times. Contains no caffeine.

Mock Tea

Put 1 tsp crushed, dried sage leaves in a teacup and cover with boiling water. Steep, strain and add a bit of lemon and a bit of herb honey.

Sage is one of the "fines herbes" and contains, of course, no caffeine.

Variation: For Fines Herbes tea, put 1/4 tsp each basil, chervil, parsley and sage in cup and follow instructions above.

GRAVIES
Mock Giblet Gravy

1. Take 1 cup of freshly cooked (by any method you prefer) chestnuts or reconstituted dried chestnuts, chop into small chunks and set aside.

2. Toast 2 oz soy flour or soy milk powder in a low (275-300°) oven, or skillet-toast over a moderately warm burner. Combine in blender with 1 tsp

food yeast, 1 cup Bumstock II, 1 tsp poultry seasoning, 1 tsp each Vegebutcher salt and soy sauce, with 1 Tbs walnut, olive or sesame oil.

3. Process til smooth, pour into saucepan and heat gently, stirring til thickened.

4. Add "giblets" (chestnut bits) and serve.

Note: Ideally, you should make your roux from chestnut flour. If you have it, substitute it for the soy flour.

Lumpy Gravy

1. Heat 1 Tbs vegetable oil and 1 lump of soy butter. Add 1 Tbs grated onion and 1 Tbs potato starch. Stir til smooth.

2. Add 1 cup of cashew-nut milk and 1/4 cup cashew lumps (put them in a waxed bag and administer a few whacks with a wooden mallet), Vegebutcher salt to taste and, for extra lumpiness, 1/4 cup of fresh "lumped" mushrooms.

3. Heat, stirring til thickened. Good over lumpy mashed potatoes, if that's one of your specialties.

Eggbeater Gravy

1. Beat 1 large egg with 2 Tbs lemon juice and 3 Tbs plain yogurt.

2. Pour hot vegetable broth or Bumstock into this mixture gradually. Return pot to heat for a few shakes of a lamb's tail (don't boil).

Greenbutcher's Gravy I

1. Blend until smooth: 2 cups of hot vegetable broth or Bumstock II, with 1 cup cashew nuts, 1 Tbs onion flakes, 1 tsp Vegebutcher salt, 1/4 tsp celery seed, 1 Tbs vegetable oil, dash of thyme, fresh chopped parsley (up to 1/2 cup).

2. Add: 1 lb of fresh, lightly steamed green peas (or thawed frozen peas).

3. Reblend and heat, stirring til thick (a pat of butter is optional at this point).

Greenbutcher's Gravy II

1. Melt 4 Tbs vegetable margarine in a saucepot and stir in 3 Tbs vegetable flour (soy, chick-pea, etc.), and 3 Tbs Vegemeat I.

2. When blended, add 3 cups of Bumstock II, stirring rapidly with a wire whisk. Cook about 20 min, stirring often.

3. Meanwhile, cut the stems from a bunch of watercress (save for making Bumstock) and drop the cress into a small saucepan of boiling water. Simmer, covered, about 30 seconds.

4. Drain, squeeze to extract liquid, and chop. Set aside (there should be about 1/3 cup).

5. Add 1 cup of heavy dairy or soy cream to sauce with salt and pepper to taste and simmer 15 mins.

6. Strain through a fine sieve, return to pan and stir in cress. Serve piping hot.

Oat Gravy

1 qt boiling water
4 oz oatmeal flour or quick oats
1 Tbs oil
1 tsp or more Insta-Steer Savory
1 tsp Vegebutcher salt

Boil oats until thickened, add oil and seasoning.

Potato-Peel Gravy

1. Chop 1 cup of potato peels and simmer for 20 mins in 1 cup of broth (or 1/2 cup broth and 1/2 cup liquid reserved from simmering vegetables used in the recipe).

2. Meanwhile, saute 1 cup of finely shredded onion in 1 Tbs vegetable oil and, when golden, stir in 1 Tbs potato flour, 1 tsp Insta-Steer Starter, and Vegebutcher salt to taste.

3. Stir til smooth and then stir in potato-peel juices.

4. Put everything in blender and process til smooth. Good with 100% Vegetarian Noodles (see ON THE SIDE) or over toast for an unbloodied, unbowed, cheap lunch.

Pea-Pod Gravy

1. Wash 1 lb of fresh peas in the pod. Shell and put the pods through a juice extractor.

2. Simmer peas in this pea-pod juice over low heat for 5 mins.

3. Combine in blender with 1 Tbs food yeast, 1/2 tsp thyme, 1/2 tsp celery salt, 1 Tbs potato starch, 1 cup buttermilk, 1 tsp Vegebutcher salt. Process til smooth. Or, you may hold out half the raw peas and add these now as you heat the gravy in a saucepan til thickened and warm enough to ladle over tonight's favorite fake steak.

Pecan-Milk Gravy

1. Combine 2 cups water, milk or soy milk with 1/3 cup raw pecans. Blend til smooth.

2. Add pinch of nutmeg and 1/3 cup of salted pecans, 1 Tbs arrowroot starch. Blend again.

3. Heat til well warmed, stirring all the while and apply as a dumpling dresser-upper.

Note: If you suspect that these gravies might also be soups thickly disguised as sauces, go to the head of the gravy-boat. Any of the last three can be converted to chowderish soups with a little bit of thinning out.

SAUCES
Horseless Horseradish

2 egg yolks, hard cooked
3 Tbs cider vinegar
2 Tbs fresh grated horseradish
1 Tbs yogurt or cream
1/2 tsp Vegebutcher salt

Rub yolks to smooth paste and gradually add vinegar. Work in grated root, cream and salt. Beat until light and fluffy.

Fin-less Fish Sauce

1. Put 1 unopened 14-oz can of sweetened condensed milk (remove label) into a large saucepan and add water to cover.

2. Bring water to a boil and simmer can, adding more water if necessary to keep can covered, for 2 hours.

3. Opoen can and in a bowl combine the now caramelized condensed milk with 2 cups of unsweetened (preferably fresh) coconut.

4. Spoon over mock fish, or sweetbreads, or spoon into tall glasses or melon halves and chill for dessert.

Moo-less Meat Sauce

1. In a saucepan, combine 1/4 cup sugar or honey, 1/4 cup Vegemeat, 1/4 cup not-so-hot chili sauce, 3/4 cup water, broth or Bumstock II, 1/4 tsp crushed red pepper.

2. In a separate bowl, blend together 1 Tbs cornstarch or arrowroot powder with 2 Tbs lime juice (lemon may be substituted); stir into bean mixture and cook over medium heat until it thickens and comes to a boil.

3. Serve at room temperature, or not, as you prefer.

Sprout Tomato Sauce

1 cup steamed sprouts (lentils, chick-peas, peas)
2 small onions
2 Tbs vegetable oil
2 cups cooked tomatoes
1 tsp soy sauce
1/2 cup chopped celery
1 cup chopped red or green pepper
2 tsp Vegebutcher salt

Fry onions in oil until browned. Add rest of ingredients, cover and simmer 10 mins.

Sprout Curry Sauce

1/2 cup minced onion
2 Tbs butter or soy butter
1 or 2 Tbs curry powder
1 cup Bumstock II
2 egg yolks
1/2 cup light cream or soy cream or plain yogurt
4 cups lentil sprouts

1. Saute onions in butter until transparent; add curry powder and stir well. Cook 2 mins and transfer to top of double-boiler.

2. Add stock, cover and simmer 10 mins over low heat.

3. After 5 mins, put sprouts in saucepan with 1/2 cup stock and simmer 5 mins.

4. Whip yolks and cream (or cream substitute) with fork and add 1/2 cup curry broth. Stir egg mixture into remainder of curry broth. Cook over hot water, stirring until mixure thickens.

5. Stir in sprouts and pour over whatever hot mockery you have waiting in the wings.

Sprouter's Postscript: If you have an onion or clove of garlic that is beginning to sprout, put it in a flower pot and let it grow into nutritious tasty greens for your salads.

"There is a trend away from fresh fruit and vegetables. According to the latest available figures on the American diet, we ate an average of four pounds less fruit and vegetables in 1972 than we did in 1971."
— USDA Researcher Dr. Ruth Burke

Steak Sauce With Seeds

1/4 cup whey or milk powder
2 cups water
1/4 cup toasted sesame seeds
1/4 cup sunflower seeds
2 tsp onion powder
2 Tbs unrefined olive or sesame oil
1/2 tsp sea salt
2 Tbs arrowroot powder

    1. Put everything in blender and process.
    2. Transfer to saucepan and stir constantly over medium flame until thickened. For a browner sauce, stir in 1 tsp instant cereal-coffee.

Steak Sauce with Nuts

2 cups water
1/2 cup cashew nuts, raw
2 Tbs arrowroot powder
2 Tbs onion flakes
2 Tbs unrefined nut oil (walnut, sesame, pumpkin)
1/2 tsp bought or Homemade Poultry Seasoning
1/2 tsp miso

    1. Grind nuts, then add remaining ingredients and process til smooth in blender.
    2. Pour into small saucepan over medium heat and cook until thickened and well warmed. Serve with any Fake Steak.

Italian Green Sauce

1 Tbs minced capers
2 mashed cloves garlic
Mock MSG II (to taste)
1 Tbs minced parsley (Italian flat-leaved preferred)
1 Tbs minced basil
1 pinch crushed rosemary
1 Tbs olive oil
2 tsp lemon juice and 1 minced twist of lemon rind
Vegebutcher salt as needed

Combine everything, tasting as you go, and pack the upshot in a nice crock for giving away or keeping around.

Italian-American Green Mayonnaise

1 large fresh egg
1/4 tsp dry mustard
1/4 tsp each oregano, basil, Italian flat-leaved parsley
1 cup olive oil
1 ripe avocado

1. Make sure all ingredients are at room temperature.
2. Put egg in blender container along with 1/4 cup oil and all the seasonings.
3. Blend on "chop" for 5 seconds, then remove cap in container cover and, with blender running, slowly add remaining oil in a steady stream. Turn blender to "liquefy" for a few seconds to incorporate any beads of oil remaining on surface.
4. Peel, seed and quarter avocado (save seed for planting) and, with blender running, add a quarter at a time, pureeing until all is smoothly blended. Makes slightly more than 1 cup pale-green mayo which you must refrigerate and to which you may add 1 or 2 Tbs chopped chives for appearance's sake.

Tartare Steak Sauce

1-1/2 cups homemade mayonnaise
1 dill pickle
4 shallots
1 Tbs each: minced, drained capers; parsley; tarragon; chervil
1 tsp prepared mustard
1 Tbs (or so) plain yogurt
1 tsp lemon juice plus sugar, salt, pepper to taste

Combine everything, correct seasoning and bottle. Serve with mock fish or Mock-Tartare steaks.

Mock Game Mustard

In a small bowl combine 1 cup dry English mustard and 1/4 tsp Vegebutcher salt. Add 1/2 cup boiling water in a stream, stirring, and continue to stir the mixture until smooth. Stir in 1/4 cup olive oil and 1-1/2 Tbs each Worcestershire sauce and cider vinegar. Let mustard cool. About 1 cup. Stir in 1 Tbs minced drained capers.

Sesame Meat Mustard

Grind 1/2 cup sesame seeds and 1 Tbs mustard seed to a powder (preferably in a seed mill). Put 1-1/2 tsp lemon juice in blender with 1 tsp oil and 6 Tbs water and 1 tsp salt. Gradually add seeds and continue blending until thick and creamy.

Soybean Mustard

2 cups soybeans sprouted 24 hours, then cooked at a very low temperature 2-3
   hours
2 medium onions, sliced and sauteed in 2 Tbs vegetable oil or soy butter
1/2 cup parsley sprigs
3 fresh sweet basil leaves (or 1/2 tsp dried basil)
1 tsp Vegebutcher salt
1 Tbs ground mustard seed
2 Tbs soy sauce

Place small amount of bean-cooking water in blender. Add 1/2 the cooked
soybeans and blend on low until coarsely ground. Add remainder of beans and
enough cooking liquid to blend to a smooth paste. Add sauteed onion, parsley,
herbs, salt, soy sauce. Should be thick and smooth and very spreadable.

There is no grading standard for pork and no
requirement for inspection of pork to detect
trichinosis. And although illegal in Den-
mark and other countries, irradiation, or ex-
posure to X-rays, is widely used to preserve
pork products in this country.
— Nikki and David Goldbeck, *The Super-
    market Handbook*, Harper & Row, 1973

ON THE SIDE

SMALL FRYS
Crisp, Edible Short-Order Garnishes

CAULIFLOWER FRY: Remove stem and hard core from a large cauliflower and separate it into flowerets. Rinse these and cook them in a kettle of boiling water (salted) for 8 mins. Drain in a colander and dry well with paper towels. Fry flowerets in hot deep oil (375°), turning them until they are golden brown and transfer to paper towels.
Serve ON THE SIDE of: Butterfly Shrimp.

RADISH FRY: Heat small amount of oil in a frying pan. Thinly slice a pound of radishes and add to oil. Sprinkle liberally with salt, Vegebutcher salt, or cumin salt. Add a pinch of tarragon and cook gently (covered) for 15 mins until radishes are pink and soft.
Serve ON THE SIDE of: Fried "Clams" for 4.

SPUD FRY: Halve one firm baking potato and chop each half into matchsticks (about 1/8" thick for quick cooking). Pour 2 or more Tbs vegetable oil into baking pan and thoroughly anoint each matchstick. Pepper with pepper, Vegebutcher salt and paprika, or you may also add a bit of hickory-smoked seasoning salt. Put pan and potatoes into a preheated 425° oven and oven-fry for 10 mins (turning once) or until crisp-brown.
Serve ON THE SIDE of: Pepper Pot for 4.

FRITTER CRITTERS: Heat a kettle of oil (2 to 3" of economical but not poor quality oil) to a boil. Add some salt and a slice of ginger to reduce odor and spatter, and quickly add squares of won ton skin, one at a time, using a pair of tongs to give them a quick twist or shaping after they hit the oil. Remove when brown and crispy, like fried chicken skin. You may also use egg roll skins (cut in three long strips, tie into bows and fry), or spring roll skins (these are disc-

shaped) cut in half and rolled into cornucopias, then dropped into the hot oil. Drain well on toweling or napkins and sprinkle with vegetable-broth powder or Vegebutcher salt, or salty poppy seeds.
Serve ON THE SIDE of: Bum Stir.

NOODLE FRY: Soak buckwheat or whole wheat noodles in cold water for 20 mins. Drain well. Deep fry in small amounts in hot oil until golden brown.
Serve ON THE SIDE of: Peking Pork.

UNDER BUMS

What to Put Under Your Next Meatless Burger, Fake Steak or Sliced Baloney

I
1. Combine 3-3/4 cups water, 1 cup long-grain rice, 2 tsp salt in saucepan.
2. Bring water to boil, reduce heat to very low and cook rice covered for 30 mins.
3. Let rice cool (it will be sticky) until it can be handled, then stir in 2 tsp soy sauce and shape the rice with dampened hands, 1/3 cup at a time, into half-inch-thick triangular cakes.
4. Line a colander with paper toweling and arrange layers of cakes in it, topped with toweling; then repeat process, ending with a paper towel layer. Put colander over pan of boiling water and steam cakes, covered with a lid, for 20 mins or until they are heated through. Makes about 12 rice crunch Under Bums. (P.S. Here's another spiffy use to put your two-piece spaghetti-cooker to.)

II
1. Melt 6 Tbs soy butter in a skillet over moderate heat and saute 2 large grated potatoes (skins and all, if organically grown) which you have squeezed nearly dry.
2. Sprinkle with 2 Tbs of Vegebutcher salt, 1/2 tsp horseradish powder and cook over a very low heat for 8 mins, flipping over at the half-way mark.
3. Beat 2 large eggs with 1/2 cup plain yogurt or buttermilk; add 1/2 cup of a whole-grain flour and beat til it becomes a smooth batter.
4. Heat 1 Tbs vegetable oil in a separate 10" skillet and pour in Under Bum batter.

5. Place in preheated 450° oven to bake 15 mins. When batter puffs up, prick with fork. Reduce heat to 350° and bake 10 mins more.

6. Place potato mixture over half the Under Bum, top with desired mock-meat and fold other half over top. Cut into 12 wedges and serve hot.

INNER BUMS
Banana Stuffing for Mock-Chicken Dishes

2 ripe bananas
4 cups slightly stale whole-grain bread
1/2 cup vegetable oil
1/3 cup each, minced celery, minced scallion
1/2 tsp Tabasco
2 Tbs lime juice
1/2 cup cashew nuts, toasted
1/2 tsp sea salt

1. Mash bananas coarsely with a fork, add lime juice and let mixture stand 5 mins.

2. Cut bread (crusts removed) into 1/4" cubes.

3. Heat oil and saute bread for 2 mins. Add nuts and vegetables and saute until mixture is soft and cubes are browned.

4. Season with salt and Tabasco.
Serve ON THE SIDE of: Mock Drum Sticks

"An acre of soybeans furnishes protein for one person for six years while the protein raised on one acre via animals would last only 77 days for one person . . ."
— *Let's Live* Magazine, Nov., 1974

CANTONESE DRESSING TO GO
(Inside Dumplings, Won Tons, Egg Rolls or Steam in Casserole Dish)

1 cup salted, squeezed, chopped greens (Chinese cabbage, mustard greens, spinach, chard, etc.)
1 cup Tofu I or scrambled eggs
1/2 cup bamboo shoots, cooked and chopped
1/4 cup soaked chooped mushrooms
2 Tbs soy sauce and 1 tsp sugar
3 Tbs cooking oil
1/4 cup stock with 1 tsp gelatin

    1. Cook broth with gelatin (mix with cold broth first, then heat).
    2. Let cool and fold in remaining ingredients.
    3. Stuff buns, eggrolls (see Bum Wraps for variations on this theme) or won ton and put into collapsible steamer in pot of boiling water with tight cover. Steam 20 mins or time required according to recipe.

Note: To boil the stuffed buns (eggrolls, etc.), omit the gelatin in above recipe. Serve on the inside of any Bum Wrap.

UPPER BUMS
Edibles to Garnish Your Stews, Steaks, and Pseudo Stroganoffs

EGG CLOUDS
Beat (fork-whip is sufficient) 2 large egg whites and boil a few inches of water, in a small saucepan. Tip in whites, lower heat by half, salt lightly, clap cover back on, and steam-cook about 3 mins. Transfer delicacy with slotted spoon to whatever waiting delicacy they are to top off.

A STEW STREUSEL (Start a day ahead)
1 cup yellow corn meal
1cup oatmeal
1 tsp salt

1 cup whole-wheat flour
1 cup finely ground bran

Mix everything and add enough water to make a stiff dough. Roll out to 1/2''
thickness. Bake in 325° oven til slightly brown. Remove and let mellow for a
day. While still a bit moist, grind up. Then add 1 cup Bumstock to 1/2 cup honey
and 1/2 cup water, mix thoroughly and sprinkle over the ground grain, but don't
over-moisten. Let partly dry, then place in a low oven to dextrinize (sweeten)
and brown. Sprinkle over stew before serving.

SZECHUAN GRINDER RELISH

12 bell peppers (half of them red, if available)
6 pounds cabbage (all one kind or mixed)
6 medium carrots and /or parsnips
6 medium onions
3 pints apple cider vinegar (a good quality)
1 cup (or somewhat less) honey, to taste
1 Tbs celery seed
1 Tbs prepared mustard
1 tsp herb seasoning, your choice
Szechuan seasoning: 1 Tbs hot pepper flakes, 2 Tbs oil, 1/8 tsp black pepper, 1/4
    tsp chili powder

    1. Grind vegetables into a bowl.
    2. Add honey, vinegar and all spices except Szechuan seasoning.
    3. Heat oil in small heavy skillet til very hot. Test readiness with one pepper
flake. If oil foams around it, quickly pour oil over remaining flakes in small cup.
Mix in pepper and chili powder. When sizzling stops, add this mixture to the
first bowl and combine well.
    4. Put relish in jars and refrigerate until needed, but postpone need for at
least one week while full flavor develops.
    Serve ON THE SIDE of: Szechuan Grinders.

RED KRAUT-RELISH
For Red-hots and Other Stuff

Wash and roughly chop:
12 red bell peppers
6 pounds red cabbage
2 large red onions

Put washed, chopped vegetables through meat grinder. Add pinch of salt, 1/2 Tbs prepared mustard, 1 tsp cayenne, 6 Tbs honey, 1 cup good cider vinegar. Seal in clean jars and refrigerate until needed. Good hot or cold. Better after a week's mellowing.
    Serve ON THE SIDE of: Red-hots.

100% VEGETARIAN NOODLES

I (Without wheat or milk)
3 eggs
1 cup soy flour
3 Tbs plain dry gelatin
1 Tbs Vegebutcher salt
3 raw spinach leaves

    1. Beat eggs in blender with spinach until well pureed.
    2. Combine flour, salt and gelatin in mixing bowl and stir well. Add eggs. Stir constantly (as gelatin softens, mixture will thicken). Stir into a noodle ball using rubber scraper. Chill in refrigerator and slice very thin with sharp knife. Boil in the usual fashion.
    Serve ON THE SIDE of: Salisbury Fake Steaks.

II (Egg free)
1/2 cup fresh zucchini
1 cup soy flour
1 cup whole-wheat flour

2 Tbs plain dry gelatin
1/4 cup arrowroot starch
1/2 cup Bumstock I or II

1. Put zucchini in blender with stock and liquefy.
2. Combine in mixing bowl with soy and wheat flours and gelatin. Stir constantly with rubber scraper until gelatin softens and mixture thickens.
3. Add half arrowroot powder with hands and put the other half in middle of noodle board.
4. Knead dough gently, incorporating all of the starch and adding more if dough is still sticky.
5. Chill in refrigerator and slice very thin with sharp knife. Boil in small amount of salted water and serve with or without sauce.

Serve ON THE SIDE of: Beefless Beef Wellington.

PHONEY PEANUTS

Soak 1 cup of lima beans overnight (dried, not fresh variety). Drain, reserving water for stock.

Deep-fry beans in tempura cooker, crock-pot, kettle, or whatever's right and handy, at a rather low heat until most of the moisture is gone. Dip out the beans and dry well. Sprinkle with Vegebutcher salt or any ground herbs.

Serve ON THE SIDE of: Chili Dogs.

POTATO BRITTLE

1 lb potatoes
6 Tbs sugar
2 Tbs vegetable oil
1 large glass bowl of iced water
oil for deep frying
2 Tbs honey
3 Tbs water

1. Cut spuds into medium-size chips. Place them in a wire basket and deep fry for 3 mins in 3 batches. Drain.
2. Gently heat sugar, honey, vegetable oil, water. Stir continuously until sugar dissolves completely. Put an asbestos pad under pan and continue to heat gently 2 more mins.
3. Add potato chips, turning them in syrup until every piece is well coated.
4. Separate chips one from another. As soon as they are detached, drop them individually into iced water, where the sudden impact of coolness causes the film of syrup over each chip to form a brittle coating. They should be retrieved quickly to prevent them from going limp. Eat at once.
Serve ON THE SIDE of: something sweet and pungent like Pineapple Pig or something not sweet at all like All Purpose Pet Chow (which turns out to be many a pet's pet treat).

SMOKEHOUSE VEGETABLES

Put some boiling water in a kettle or canner and toss in some scraps of smoked cheese (and/or pork and hotdog bits from departed repasts); heavily pepper the waters with hickory salt, put in your portable steamer, pile in assorted fresh stew vegetables such as carrots, string beans, cauliflower, quartered onions and potatoes, etc.; cover tightly and steam-cook for 15 mins. Vegetables will take on a smoky, meaty flavor and, combined with steamed rice, make a meal in themselves without further ado.
Serve ON THE SIDE of: Braised Spare Ribs.

FAKE PFANNKUCHEN

Take one loaf of day-old bread (pumpernickel or sourdough), slice off heels and shave off very thin slices of the rest of the loaf into a large mixing bowl (a whole loaf will yield about 4 qts of shavings). Add 3 cloves of pressed or minced garlic, 1/2 cup of freshly chopped parsley, 1 tsp each: Vegebutcher salt, pepper, vegetable broth concentrate; 1/2 tsp powdered mustard. Mix together and gradually sprinkle with 1 cup of lukewarm Bumstock II or water until evenly dampened. Cover tightly for at least 30 mins. To cook, heat garlic-flavored oil in a frying pan and scoop 2-3 cups of mixture at a time in 1/4" thick rounds. Drizzle with more oil during cooking. Turn and repeat. Cook til crisp and brown on each side.
  Serve ON THE SIDE of: Hangtown Hoax.

COW COW CHOW CHOW
Chewy-chewy Burger Relish

4 cups coarsely chopped celery or fennel
1 cup chopped green peppers
1 cup chopped red peppers
1/2 cup chopped broccoli
1/2 cup wine vinegar
1 Tbs mixed pickling spice
1/4 cup honey
1 Tbs Vegebutcher salt
1 tsp caraway seed

  1. Chop vegetables coarsely, using blender or coarse knife of food grinder. Place in mixing bowl and set aside.
  2. Combine vinegar and pickling spices in saucepan. Boil five mins. Strain and add remaining ingredients. Pour over vegetables.
  3. Cover and let stew by itself in a good cold place for at least a day.
  4. Ladle into a large jar or two smaller relish glasses. Refrigerate between spreading and snacking.
  Serve ON THE SIDE of: Under Dogs or any burger, or on plain cottage cheese. Makes insipid soups less so. Super dessert for sourpusses.

175

HERBED COCONUT

Cut a fresh coconut into bite-sized pieces. Place them in a shallow baking pan and dry them slowly in a 200° oven. Turn into bowl and add 1/2 tsp each: garlic flakes, paprika, kelp, Vegebutcher salt, and 1 tsp Homemade Poultry Seasoning. Coat coconut pieces well and store in tightly closed tins or jars.
    Serve ON THE SIDE of: Banana Fish.

HERBED CABBAGE

1 cup cabbage pulp (if you have a juicer) or 1 cup shredded cabbage
4 Tbs vinegar
1/2 tsp each: summer savory, dill seed, Vegebutcher salt, caraway seed

Place the works in a covered refrigerator dish or casserole and let age for 3 or 4 days (the longer the aging, the better the overall flavor). Good for whatever ails you. Good with whatever delights you.
    Serve ON THE SIDE of: Phoney Baloney

HERBED BOTTLE GREENS

Keep three big bottles (pickle jars, Mason jars, etc.) of sprouts going at all times — a bean, a grain, and a small seed — whose protein patterns complement each other. To serve, combine a handful of each, toss with hand-made salad dressing, home-grown (hopefully) herbs and serve with anything. No food fits the description of a Unifood better than sprouts.
    Serve ON THE SIDE of: Bum Stew I.

WOK POPS

Heat 2 Tbs of a tasty non-animal oil in a wok (or skillet) til hot but not smoking. Stir in 1/2 cup of whole-wheat berries and stir-fry for less than a min. Cover and whisk away from heat. The wheat will pop like corn and may be eaten with a salting of whatever herb has the topnote in your Mock-meat dish.

Serve ON THE SIDE of: Rolled Rump of Peanut, for instance, powdered with bell pepper salt (grind some pepper flakes).

MOCK POPPED CORN

Heat 2 Tbs vegetable oil (not olive oil) in a wok (or skillet) and when not quite smoking-hot, stir in 1/2 cup of whole unpolished brown, long-grain rice (you may dilute with some Italian orzo or raw long-grain rice) and stir-fry over high heat 30 seconds. Slap on a tight-fitting cover and whisk off heat. While sitting idle, grains will pop and puff.

Serve ON THE SIDE of: Bumstead Juniors with a nesting of fresh home-grown turnip greens.

CRACKLINGS
A Crunchy Counterfeit

2 sheets of egg roll skin
oil for deep frying
Mock MSG or Vegebutcher salt

Bring egg roll skins to room temperature (but do not allow them to expire or they will be unmanageable) and cut into four long bands. Put two bands at a time into a kettle of boiling oil (if you added salt and some sliced ginger you will have less spatter and smell) forming into loose circles just before you do. Or you may twist the strips slightly instead for a long bow-tie effect. Fry until golden brown and crusty. Remove with tongs and drain on paper toweling. Season with Vegebutcher salt or Mock MSG. Eat as is, or serve as called for.

PICKLED HEART

Halve 12 medium-sized celery hearts and 6 hearts of fresh fennel (or you may use all celery heart). Combine 1 tsp whole celery seed, 1 Tbs mustard see, 1/2 tsp garlic powder, 1/4 cup thick honey, 1/2 cup water, 1 cup cider vinegar. Tie into a spice bag (cheesecloth sachet), 1 tsp whole black pepper, 1/4 tsp each whole allspice and whole cloves and add to first mixture. Bring to boiling point and boil 1 min. Add celery hearts and fennel hearts and bring to a second boil. Remove spice bag (save to use again), pack in sterilized jars and seal at once.
Serve ON THE SIDE of: Szechuan Grinder.

PICKLED HEAD

Simmer 3 cups vinegar with 2 Tbs mustard seed, 3/4 cup honey, 8 cloves, 4 sticks cinnamon. Break 2 heads of cauliflower into curds of equal size and cook them in a small amount of boiling water for 4 mins. Drain and put them into jars, pour pickling juice over curds and seal.
Serve ON THE SIDE of: Garden Patch Pork.

PICKLED EARS

Husk, wash and scrub free of silk 2 lbs of midget or bantam corn (failing them, you can break normal-sized ears into thirds). Then, combine 2 cups of cider vinegar with 1 cup water, 4 Tbs honey, 1 minced clove garlic and 2 small bay leaves. Bring mixture to boiling point, add corn ears and simmer 5 mins. Spoon corn ears into canning jars, pour in marinade. Seal jars immediately and enjoy, after they are good and pickled. For gift-giving, and as a special addition to salads and chop suey-type dishes.
Serve ON THE SIDE of: Pineapple Pig.

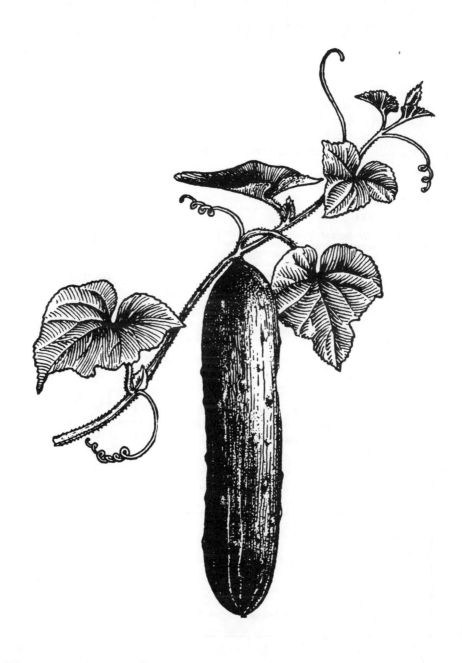

1/2 head lettuce
1 small onion
4 to 6 mint leaves
1 tsp, plus 1 oz, butter or mock butter
1 tsp flour
8 oz tiny peas (fresh or frozen)
2 Tbs cold water
1/2 tsp sugar
2 Tbs heavy dairy or soy cream
salt and pepper

1. Shred lettuce as fine as thread. Finely chop onion. Chop mint.
2. Work the 1 tsp butter and 1 tsp flour into a paste on a small saucer. Melt the ounce of butter in a heavy-bottomed pan without letting it color. Add onion and lower heat. Cover pan and steam onion but do not let it burn or brown.
3. When onion is soft, add the peas and shake the pan over a low heat until the peas are just tender and still a good color.
4. Add shredded lettuce and water. Continue to shake pan for 2-3 mins. Season lightly with mint, salt, pepper, sugar.
5. Whisk in small amounts of the butter paste, letting liquid thicken after each addition. Add cream before mixture gets too thick. Heat til warm.
   Serve ON THE SIDE of: Burger Bits or Good Red Meat.

> "DDE is one trace of DDT which food technologists expect to show up in milk and other foods for the next decade or two. And Dieldrin is still in use for that persistent pesticide is on corn crops, an important constitutent of cow fodder."
> *Consumer Reports*, Jan., '73

SCATTER GOODS

2 lbs broccoli
6 dried Chinese mushrooms (optional)
1 cup shredded celery stalks (fennel may be substituted)
2 Tbs peanut oil
1 tsp Vegebutcher salt
1/4 tsp sugar
1/4 tsp almonds
1 tsp arrowroot or cornstarch dissolved in 1 Tbs Bumstock (I or II, whichever is appropriate)

    1. Wash broccoli and cut flowers from stems in clusters.
    2. Peel stems by cutting 1/8'' into skin and stripping down as you would peel an onion (reserve peelings for soup). Slice stalks diagonally into 1'' pieces.
    3. Cover mushrooms with 1/2 cup warm water and soak 1/2 hour. Drain, reserving liquid. Quarter mushrooms. Shred celery.
    4. Set 10'' skillet or 12'' wok over medium heat for 30 seconds. Pour in oil and heat 30 seconds. Add broccoli and shredded celery. Stir-fry 1 min. Add broccoli buds and stir-fry 1 more min.
    5. Add honey, salt, reserved mushroom liquid, mushrooms, almonds. Stir briefly, cover and cook over moderate heat 2-3 mins. Stir cornstarch mixture to recombine and pour into pan. Stir until vegetables are coated with a light clear glaze.
    Serve ON THE SIDE of: Mocking Birds I or II, maybe?

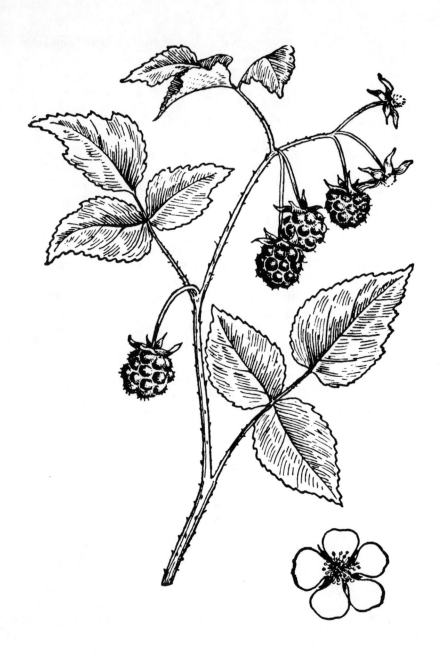

DAIRYLESS DESSERTS

MOO-LESS RICE PUDDING
No Eggs, No Milk

1/2-3/4 cup glutinous rice or short-grain rice or combination of barley and any rice
1/4 cup red beans (i.e., aduki or kidney)
4-1/2 cups water
1 cup mixed fruits and nuts (glazed if you like) including dates, almonds, peanuts, sugared ginger, etc.
4 Tbs honey and 1 Tbs date or brown sugar

    1. Wash rice (and barley if used) and place in a heavy pot with beans. Add water and bring to a boil.
    2. Turn heat as low as possible and place pot on an asbestos pad, putting both of these on burner.
    3. Stir at 15 min intervals. After 45 mins, add fruits and nuts. Simmer gently for another hour, stirring at 20 min intervals. Spoon in honey and sugar and pour into dessert cups. Luscious, moo-less, hot or cold.

COW TOW
Cowless Milk Candy

Combine 1/4 cup arrowroot starch with 1/4 cup soy milk powder, a dash of vanilla extract, 1 beaten egg white, and a handful of chopped nuts or Grainola (optional). Knead slightly on waxed paper. Press into a pre-floured (with soy milk powder or arrowroot) glass dish or small, square Pyrex pan. Impress surface with "cow toes" (walnut halves) if you like. Chill before slicing into squares or bars.

JERSEY BOUNCE
A Moo-juice-less Junket

2 cups soy milk
2 Tbs honey
pinch nutmeg
1 tsp any pure flavoring extract
1 junket tablet and 1 Tbs cold water

1. Place junket tablet in cold water and crush to dissolve.
2. Heat soy milk to 110°, stir in honey, extract and junket mixture only until well combined. Pour immediately into dessert cups and, after 10 mins of standing, chill.

BUM BOMBE
Egg-less, Cream-free

2 cups freshly made soy cream blended with 2 Tbs plain gelatin
2-3 boxes fresh strawberries
honey
2 cups fresh or canned pineapple, well drained

1. Mix soy cream with strawberries in blender at high speed, slowly adding honey until taste becomes quite sweet. Pour into a bombe mold, pre-rinsed with cold water. Freeze til nearly firm.
2. Combine pineapple with remaining cream and blend as in Step 1, adding honey again til sweet enough. Pour into mold atop strawberry cream and freeze again. Unmold when solid.

BUM BOMBE SHELL
Yolk-less and Lard-less

4 egg whites
1/4 tsp cream of tartar
1/3 cup raw or date sugar

1. Beat whites with cream of tartar until stiff. Continue beating and gradually add sugar.

2. Spoon misture into pie pan or ovenproof bombe shell and spread evenly over bottom and along sides of pan or mold.

3. Bake in 350° oven 12-15 mins until delicately browned. Good with above ice cream inside — or nothing fancier than thick applesauce.

MOCK-MILK CHOCOLATES

3 cups water
1/2 cup honey
2 cups raw sugar
1 lb skinned chestnuts

1. Put water in heavy saucepan and dissolve sugar and honey in it over very low heat. When all sugar has dissolved and liquid becomes syrup-like, add chestnuts.

2. Put an asbestos pad under pan and cook steadily for 45-60 mins over gentle heat, turning chestnuts over now and then til glazed and chewy. Serve or save in fluted foil candy cups.

"Meat," says the *British Medical Journal*, "is the main source of 'acid ash' in the fluid surrounding the body's cells and this condition increases the bones' tendency to lose minerals."

185

TWO 100% VEGETARIAN ICE CREAMS
Eggless, milkless

I
1/2 cup crushed, drained raspberries or strawberries
1/4 cup soy powder
1/4 cup honey
1-1/2 trays ice cubes
1 cup water or berry juice
1 ripe banana
1 Tbs vegetable oil

1. Blend all ingredients except ice cubes. Put blender container in refrigerator.
2. After 1/2 hour, remove container and, with blender running, add ice cubes rapidly. As mixture thickens, add last few cubes slowly.
3. Pour into freezer trays and put in freezer.
4. For extra smoothness, you may whip in blender after ice cream has reached "mush" stage, then refreeze.

II
1/2 cup chilled honey
2 cups frozen yogurt
1-1/2 cups frozen pineapple pieces
2 frozen bananas, sliced
1 cup frozen Mock Cream
1 tsp vanilla extract
1/2 tsp lemon juice

Put ingredients in blender in order given. Liquefy on low speed, using rubber scraper to scrape down sides. When finished, dessert will be very cold, very thick and creamy and ready to eat in very cold cups.

COWLESS CUSTARD

1 cup Mock Milk
2 Tbs molasses or honey
1/2 tsp cinnamon
2 eggs
pinch sea salt
1/2 tsp vanilla extract

    1. Beat eggs slightly. Mix in other ingredients. Pour into custard dishes. Place dishes in pan of hot water.
    2. Bake at 325° for 50 mins. A table knife inserted in the custard should come out cleanly when the custard is done. Makes two lady-like servings.

Chemical Growth promoters go on. Following the Government's ban on the cattle-fattening hormone DES (which was shown in tests with laboratory animals to be cancer-causative), two new synthetic hormones are now being made available to cattlemen — MGA, used on heifers, and Zeranol, a chemical which effectively fattens steers and lamb before the kill. Their safety, according to experts, has yet to be demonstrated.

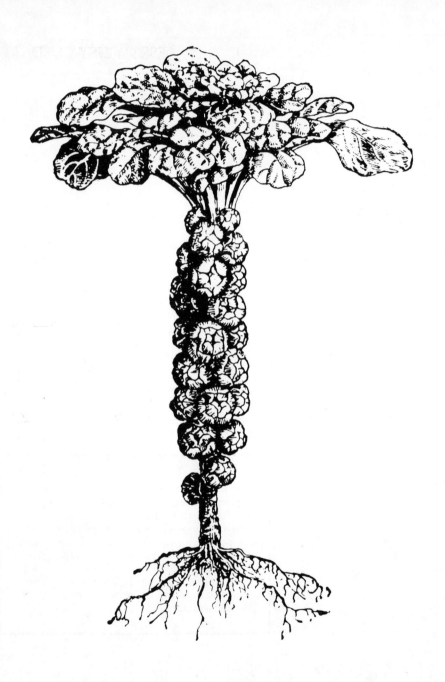

STEERAGE

BUMMERS
The Vegebutcher's Blunder-Mender and Leftovers Guide

1. The Tofu did not "jell" enough. You can put this soup-like soy cheese in the blender with some pectin (use 1 tsp of the sugarfree kind per cup of cheese) and some sweetening (1 or 2 Tbs honey per cup), process briefly, put half the mixture in a saucepot over medium heat and stir til thoroughly warmed and thickened a bit. Blend again and pour into dessert cups for a high-protein, low-calorie pudding.

2. The Gluten (which you prepared and stored without bath water in the refrigerator) is now tough as beef jerky. Forget the stew you were going to make, put the chunks through the food grinder along with some fresh herbs and a few vegetable chunks (raw), then combine with one whipped egg white, and wheat germ to counteract excess wetness (mixture should be light and moist). Shape into balls and run lightly through some wheat germ. Place in lightly oiled steamer basket over boiling water and steam-cook in covered pot 15 mins. Sauce it and serve.

3. The Gluten steaks over-baked, leading even the most confirmed agrarian-vegetarian to thoughts of big whoppers. Before that happens, put the steaks through your meat grinder til you have a nice bowl of kibble. Combine with a sauce or gravy and serve over toast or waffles. Or, mince very small, sauce, and serve.

4. Unjelled Jelly Fish? Worse, it is only half-jelled, no good for drinking or dunking. So, you simply heat up a cup of it, then cool to warm, and sprinkle with 1 Tbs baking yeast and you have the beginnings of a beautiful loaf of bread or pan of buns.

5. You overcooked the rice, thereby creating a nice snack by-product. Scrape the rice crust out of the paan, combine with some tempura batter and drop by small balls into hot oil. Fry two mins, cool and crunch.

6. You made Tofu and hadn't counted on all that whey. Why not Milky Whey Jello? Dissolve 2 packets of plain gelatin in 1/4 cup cold whey and , when clear, combine with 2 cups more whey and heat this, stirring carefully until it is up to a boil. Put in the blender with 1 tsp alginate powder (this nutrifies and thickens) and 3 Tbs of any natural sweetener. Pour into custard cups or parfait glasses and chill thoroughly til jelled.

7. Leftover Wheat Loaf? Cut into squares and stir into a Sprout Sauce for another meal. And if that meal is more than a tomorrow away, put the sauced Wheat Loaf squares in cold wraps and freeze. Or, crumble Wheat Loaf remains and use in place of breadcrumbs in any meatloaf recipe or wherever Vegemeat is called for.

8. Your Wok Pops pooped out in mid-pop? There is always a batch that disappoints due to quality of oil, temperature of wok or temperament of the grains themselves. Put these brown berries into the seed mill or blender and half-pulverize. Combine with your homemade bread crumbs and use wherever breading or crumbs are called for. Or mix a bit into your Grainola canister if it seems oversweet.

9. Your Mock Mac or Sham Lamb Burger did not cohere as expected and you are eggless? Mince some prepared Gluten and combine with your burger bits. Crumble-proofing.

10. The pulp from the home-manufacture of Tofu is a very usable discard. For instance, combine with your canned dog food as a nutrition booster and meat stretcher. But to be fully digestible, give it a 20 min processing in your pressure cooker.

11. Never view your leftovers as so much distressed merchandise. An oversupply of sesame mustard, for instance, is half the battle of hors d'oeuvre-making. Thicken a bit with more ground sesame and stuff into 4" lengths of celery, fennel or rhubarb.

12. Made more nutmeal than you needed? Save and use to thicken sauces and gravies as they do in Africa (with peanuts) and Asia (with macadamias).

And when all else fails. . .
VEGEBUTCHER BLUNDER BLENDER COMPOST
Put the burned beans, the uncongealed bean curd, the failed Gluten, the sour Mock-lox, or what have you, into the blender with whatever vegetable scrapings, egg shells, rejected gravy, apple cores and coffee grounds you also have and buzz the works. Dump some now and then on hungry, needy houseplants.

SENDING AWAY FOR STUFF

Herbs and Spices
Rocky Hollow Herb Farm
Box 215
Lake Wallkill Road
Sussex, N.J. 07461

Complete Mushroom Growing Kits
Mushroom Supply Co.
Toughkenamon, Pa. 19374

Sausage Casings (natural)
Rebecca Adams/Jack McGuire
20 North Wacker Drive
Chicago, Ill. 60606

Molds, Animal Cutters, Aspic Pans, Steamers, Tools, Etc.
Wilson Enterprises
833 West 115th Street
Chicago, Ill. 60643
(catalog available)

Pots & Pans Used by the Pros; Very Assorted and Unusual Wares
The Bridge Company
212 East 52nd Street
New York, N.Y. 10022

Herbs, Spices, Oils, Whole Grains, Flours, Seaweeds and More
Walnut Acres
Penns Creek, Pa. 17862

Unusual Beans and Herbs from Europe;
also Salsify (Oyster Plant) and Some Oriental Vegetables and Seeds
Le Jardin du Gourmet
Ramsey, N.J. 07446

Pollen (see REMEDY BAR for Notes), Herbs and Roots
Wonder Natural Foods
11711 Redwood Highway
Wonder, Oregon 97543

Organic Sea Products
Dorothy Page
P.O. Box 117
Sun City, Calif. 92281

Seaweeds and General Goods; Grains, Beans, Vegetables, Seeds, Much More
Erewhon Trading Co.
342 Newbury St.
Boston, Mass. 02115

Shiloh Farms
Route 59, Box 97
Sulphur Springs, Ark. 72768

Cereals, Grains, Flours (Organic)
Arrowhead Mills
Box 866
Hereford, Texas 79045

Herbs, Spices, Teas, Cheese and Cheesemaking Supplies
Homecrafts
111 Stratford Road
Winston-Salem, N.C. 27104

Milk-free Yogurt Culture (Trade Names: Soyadophilus and Theradophilus)
Dynamic Nutritional Products
P.O. Box 528
North Hollywood, Calif. 91603

Oriental seeds for planting, sprouting
Oriental Country Store
12 Mott Street
New York, N.Y. 10013

Unusual herbs, spices, botanicals. Almanac-type catalog worth writing for
Indiana Botanical Gardens
Hammond, Indiana 46325

For more names, address, sources, see: THE ORGANIC DIRECTORY
Rodale Press, Emmaus, Pa. 18049

BUM STEERS REMEDY BAR
Spuds for Stings

Raw potato meat will alleviate the pain of bee stings and fly bites as effectively as most chemical nostrums. Isn't that a-peeling?

Calcium without Bones

Good calcium source for the non-bone eating vegan: take a raw egg with the shell intact and place it in a glass of white vinegar. After several days the shell will dissolve and the egg can be tossed. Pour the remaining liquid into a qt of water, add honey and lemon (even a banana if you have one) and put through the blender. Chill. Calcium in a natural soluble state, no bones about it.

Pneumonia-proofing

Soy lecithin, a by-product of the bean sold commercially in liquid, powder or granule form, provides the virus-infected with greater resistance, and if anything more can be asked of a mock meat, it also seems, in some quarters, to immunize against pneumonia. Nothing to sneeze at.

Penicillin by the Clove

Garlic, celebrated as a good liver cleanser (and so too, beets) and for its ability to clear up congestion due to colds and even pneumonia, is known in Cossack circles as "Russian Penicillin". Because it is a powerful germ killer, it has an antiseptic effect on the intestines and helps to purify them of toxins. This, according to Dr. G. Piotrowski of the University of Geneva, accounts for its ability sometimes to reduce excessively high blood pressure.

Mexican Medicine

Non-liver lovers can turn to the chili pepper for a potent source of vitamin A to match beef liver. According to Dr. Lora M. Shields of New Mexico Highlands University, chili pepper-based food, as eaten in New Mexico, can run well over 100,000 units of that nutrient. Furthermore, her investigations indicated that chili apparently has the ability to help lower blood-fat levels, thereby reducing the risk of heart attack. Something for the vegetarian to slap on his next shiner.

Building Better Bones and Teeth by Bee

What's the most complete and potent protein food on earth? Milk, eggs, organ meats? Wrong. It's bees' pollen, according to the late Leo C. Antles. Considered the world's foremost authority on gathering and curing fruit pollen and the first person to market pollen to fruit growers, horticulturist Antles pointed out that the protein, fat, phosphorus and iron content of the nutrient most closely resembled dried kidney and navy beans and lentils. Pollen, however, is far richer than any of these in calcium and magnesium, as well as copper, riboflavin and pantothenic acid.

Million Dollar Mask

A facial treatment with all the protein, B vitamins and minerals of meat, plus some bonus minerals rarely found on the hoof: mix 2 tsp of soy or sesame yogurt into 1 tsp dried brewers yeast (add more yogurt if needed) to make a spreadable paste. Pat onto face, let harden completely, remove 20 min later with warm water. Moisturize skin with a Tbs soy oil.

DOING BUM SUMS
Completing Incomplete Proteins

1. 3/4 cup beans + 2 cups rice = 10 oz steak
2. 1/2 cup soybeans + 3 cups rice = 9 oz steak
3. 1 cup rice + 3/4 cup cracked-wheat (bulgur) + 2/3 cup soybeans = 11 oz steak
4. 1/4 cup food yeast + 1 cup whole barley = 6 oz hamburger
5. 1/2 cup sesame seeds + 1-1/2 cups millet = 3/4 cup meatballs
6. 1/3 cup soy grits + 1/2 cup sesame butter + 3/4 cup peanuts = two 5 oz beef patties
7. 1/2 cup cornmeal + 3/4 cup milk + 1/2 cup soybeans = 8 oz hamburger steak
8. 1/2 cup chick-peas + 3/4 cup sunflower seeds = 6 oz hamburger
9. 1/2 cup peanut butter + 2 cups whole wheat + 2 oz soy cream = two 6 oz minute steaks
10. 1/2 cup Tofu + 1/2 cup sesame-sunflower butter + 1/2 cup peanut meal = 8 oz round steak

PROTEIN FINDER
Vegetables, per average serving, 3-1/2 oz. uncooked

	Total Protein	Usable Protein
Lima Beans, green	8 grams	4 grams
Soybean sprouts	6	3
Peas, green, shelled	6	3
Brussels sprouts	5	3
Corn, 1 med. ear	4	3
Broccoli, 1 stalk	4	2-3
Kale, stems, cooked	4	2
Collards, cooked	4	2
Mushrooms	3	2
Asparagus	3	1.8
Artichoke	3	1.8
Cauliflower	3	1.8
Spinach	3	1.5
Turnip greens, cooked	3	1.4
Mung bean sprouts	4	1.4
Mustard greens	3	1.4
Potato, white, baked	2	1.2
Okra	2	1.2
Chard	2	1

Cereals & Grains: Per Average Serving

	Total Protein	Usable Protein
Wheat, whole grain hard red spring, 1/3 c.	8 grams	5 grams
Rye, whole grain 1/3 c.	7	4
Egg noodles, cooked 1 c.	7	4
Bulgur (parboiled wheat), 1/3 c., or cracked wheat cereal 1/3 c.	6	4
Barley, pot or scotch, 1/3 c.	6	4
Millet, 1/3 c.	6	3
Spaghetti or macaroni cooked 1 c.	5	3
Oatmeal, 1/3 c.	4	3
Rice, 1/3 c.		
a. brown	5	3
b. parboiled (converted)	5	3
c. Milled, polished	4	2
Wheat germ, commercial 2 level Tbs	3	2
Bread, commercial, 1 slice, whole-wheat or rye	2.4	1.2
Wheat bran, crude, 2 rounded Tbs	1.6	0.9

One Cup of Flour

	Total Protein	Usable Protein
Soybean flour, defatted	65 grams	40 grams
Gluten flour	85	23
Peanut flour, defatted	48	21
Soybean flour, full fat	26	16
Whole wheat flour or cracked wheat cereal	16	10
Rye flour, dark	16	9
Buckwheat flour, dark	12	8
Oatmeal	11	7
Barley flour	11	7
Cornmeal, whole ground	10	5
Wheat bran, crude	9	5

Seeds and Nuts per 1 Ounce

	Total Protein	Usable Protein
Pignolia nuts	9 grams	5 grams
Pumpkin/squash seeds	8	5
Sunflower seeds (3 Tbs) or meal (4 Tbs)	7	4
Peanuts	8	3
Peanut butter	8	3
Cashews	5	3

Recently approved by the USDA: a patented process that automatically sprays freshly dressed animal carcasses with a chlorine solution containing 40 times more chlorine than that permitted in drinking water.

COMPOSITION OF NUTS AND DRIED FRUITS

NUTS	Water	Pro-tein	Carbo-hydrate	Fat	Min-erals
Acorns	4.10	8.10	48.00	37.40	2.40
Almonds	4.90	21.40	16.80	54.40	2.50
Beechnuts	9.90	21.70	19.20	42.50	3.86
Brazil nuts	4.70	17.40	5.70	65.00	3.30
Butternuts	4.50	27.90	3.40	61.20	3.00
Candlenuts	5.90	21.40	4.90	61.70	3.30
Chestnuts (dried)	5.90	10.70	74.20	7.00	2.20
Chufa	2.20	3.50	60.70	31.60	2.00
Coconut	14.10	5.70	27.90	50.60	1.70
Filberts	5.40	16.50	11.70	64.00	2.40
Hickory nuts	3.70	15.40	11.40	67.40	2.10
Paradise nuts	2.30	22.20	10.20	62.60	2.70
Pecans	3.40	12.10	8.50	70.70	1.60
Pignons	3.40	14.60	17.30	61.90	2.90
Pignolias	6.20	33.90	7.90	48.20	3.80
Pistachios	4.20	22.60	15.60	54.56	3.10
Black Walnuts	2.50	27.60	11.70	56.30	1.90
English Walnuts	2.50	18.40	13.00	64.40	1.70
Water Chestnuts	12.30	4.00	50.00	1.20	1.77
Peanuts	7.40	29.80	14.70	43.50	2.25
Peanut Butter	2.10	29.30	17.10	46.50	2.20
Almond Butter	2.20	21.70	11.60	61.50	3.00
DRIED FRUITS					
Apples	26.10	1.60	62.00	2.20	2.00
Apricots	29.40	4.70	62.50	1.00	2.40
Pears	16.50	2.80	66.00	5.40	2.40
Peaches	20.00	3.15	50.00	.45	2.15
Prunes	22.30	2.10	71.20	—	2.30
Raisins	14.60	2.60	73.60	3.30	3.40
Currants	17.20	2.40	74.20	1.70	4.50

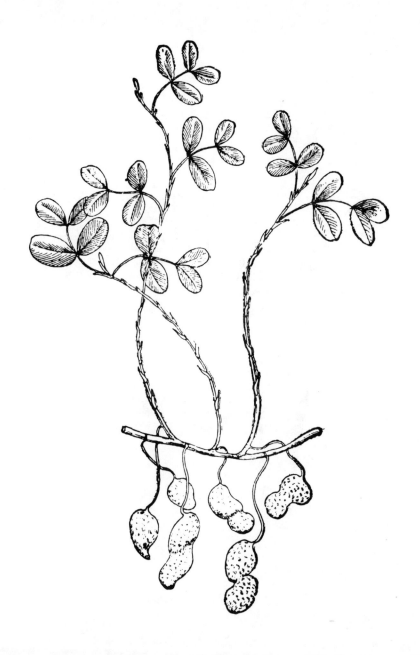

RECIPE INDEX